RUN TO WIN!

HOW YOU CAN RUN A SUCCESSFUL CAMPAIGN FOR LOCAL OR STATE PUBLIC OFFICE

by

Earl Baker

authorHOUSE®

AuthorHouse™
1663 Liberty Drive
Bloomington, IN 47403
www.authorhouse.com
Phone: 1-800-839-8640

Published by AuthorHouse 7/3/2012

ISBN: 978-1-4772-1213-4 (e)
ISBN: 978-1-4772-1214-1 (sc)

Library of Congress Control Number: 2012909369

This book is printed on acid-free paper.

Table of Contents

Introduction

"Running To Win"

Run To Win! is designed to get <u>you</u> elected!

You may be thinking about running for office, or you may already have decided to definitely run. You may be a man or a woman, you may be younger or more mature, you may live in a city, a suburban area or a rural area. The offices you might be considering running for, whether it's mayor of your town, council member, township supervisor, or a local judgeship or state representative, in all of these races you will be doing a lot of these activities yourself. Hopefully if you cover a large or populous area you'll have professional help, a staff, or at least a large number of volunteers to help you, *but you yourself need to know all the tasks that in any campaign need to be performed.* While I'm writing this to you as the candidate, the information is equally useful for your campaign manager, share it with him or her, and your campaign workers.

This book came about originally because a friend of mine who had decided to run for a local judgeship, but who had never run before, called and asked if I'd spend a Sunday afternoon with him, telling him how to run and how to win. Perhaps like you, he was a good citizen who voted and already knew in general about the local political system, well qualified, motivated to be a good judge. But he knew that he *didn't* know how to get elected. I did meet with him... and he went on to win. But it made me ask myself, how many good people are there are out there who are qualified and interested but who don't know the mechanics of running for office? Those who would value the information they could gain from my sharing the essentials of what I've learned in 20 years in politics.

Some of what you read in this book might perhaps strike you as elementary or as just plain common sense. Maybe you've run before, maybe you're already in office and just want to brush up, and that's okay. Accept these ideas as such, but since almost everything I talk about here is the result of questions candidates have asked me over the years, I figure it's better to cover everything and let the reader decide the significance of each suggestion. **A reviewer of this program once called it a "Heloise's Hints" for candidates and I like that: practical details, sometimes fairly simple, which add up to efficiency...or in our case, victory!**

Chapter One

Becoming A Candidate

Let's talk about **you** running for public office. Are you one of the estimated one million people in the United States who will run for public office in your town, city, county or district over the next few years, or are you thinking about it? In either case, this program is designed for you. I'm going to tell you how to decide about your candidacy and then how you can run to win your election. Living in a system of democracy, you might think running for office comes naturally. Well, it doesn't. It is something that we have to learn, and that's why, whether you've run before or have been thinking about running for a long time; whether you've already participated in the process, or you're brand new and are considering whether to enter the fray; it's going to help you to learn what this book and the program it outlines covers.

Let's get right down to business. What are the things you need to think of before you can decide whether or not to run for office? You may think that in politics, you must have a certain kind of personality, or to behave in a certain way. Not true. There are some things you will want to be able to do to help you get elected, and to function in the political process. But no matter what your personality, no matter what your personality type, you can be elected.

In my experience, the things that help people get elected can be summarized as follows: **a strong desire to run, a strong feeling that your ideas will be useful and helpful to the public, a willingness to listen and respect the opinions of others, as well as a supportive family, a knowledge of the issues involved, and understanding the expectations of the office which you are seeking.** And let's add to that some friends, some help from other people who are committed to you and who may know or learn about the political process. And we can also say, some luck. But you know the old saying, "Those who work hard are ready to take advantage of good luck when it comes."

Whether you're interested in running for mayor, city council, township supervisor, county commissioner or the many other local, county and authority offices, state legislature or even Congress, this program will be helpful. Chances are though, if you're thinking of running for offices such as governor or US senator or a hotly contested congressional or statewide office, you'll raise enough money to hire an expensive consultant who will give you advice and be able to spend a lot of money on your behalf. But if you are the typical candidate, running for the other offices I've talked about, chances are you don't have a lot to spend on the campaign, or on a campaign staff. However, you can get professional advice, in Run To Win!, from me. I am someone who has run for office, who has led or participated in many other campaigns, and who will share all the ideas I have learned and observed, with you. I have run for public office sixteen times, winning each time, running at the local level in my town, my county and at the state level. I've also worked on numerous other campaigns, for governor, for judge, presidential races, as well as town and county races. What I've gleaned from all those races over the past 20 years, I want to put at your disposal.

I really believe strongly that good people should run for public office. I believe that many people who would make great candidates, perhaps like you, are hesitant to get into the public arena, either because they're not sure they want to be in politics, or because they don't know how to run a winning campaign. **Only you can answer the first question as to whether you are willing to step forward and make the commitment to public life that politics requires. Maybe you already have. And if you have that commitment, I can help you with the techniques for getting elected.**

To begin with, think about this question: *why do I want to run for public office*? When you run, that will be the question that you'll hear more than any other. "Why are you running?" Chances are, you may have various motivations. Perhaps an issue or several issues have motivated you strongly to want to win people over to your way of thinking. Maybe you feel that better management is needed in your city, school district, town or county, that someone with leadership, someone that people trust, should step forward, and that you may fulfill those expectations.

One of the things that you're going to learn is that in politics, you may be put in a position where talking about your own strengths, your own desire to serve, will be very important. It might be a little uncomfortable for you, but remember, our political system is a democracy. It requires that people step forward. If you sound hesitant, if you're not sure, people

3

will sense that. So let's start off with the assumption that if you're going to go into politics, you're going to do it effectively and you're going to be proud that you are willing to serve.

Next think about this question: can you afford it? By this, I don't just mean money, although you do have to have a living that you and your family are comfortable with, and the ability to continue that while you are running, and even after you've been elected. But I also mean, do you have the time, do you have the family support? Does your wife, your husband, your children, support you in this effort? Will they resent the time that politics takes? Do you have the health, do you have the energy? I raise these questions because they are a kind of check-off list of things for you to consider. If you're not sure about the answers to these questions, sit down and discuss them with a good friend, or sit down by yourself with a paper and pencil if you work better that way. Think through these questions so that you're confident of your answers. And if the answer is yes, then let's get right into it. Let's talk about how you can run to win!

Chapter Two

Structuring Your Campaign

Campaign Plan + Organization + Meetings + Strategies + Legal/Financial

While it may sound simple and even elementary, we need to start with this goal. How can you get more votes than your opponents?

There are many answers to this question. Some of those answers have to do with who, among all the possible voters, is actually going to turn out to vote. Other answers have to do with whether it is a primary or general election, or a municipal or broader election. And some pretty important answers have to do with *how you can get people to want to vote for you.* Finally, some of the answers to this question, "How can I get more votes than my opponent?" have to do with the **steps that you can take positively to win people over, to get them committed, and to have them turn out to vote.**

Remember, in politics, **all your sales are made on one day**. You can plan, you can campaign, you can do all the

5

things we talk about in this program. But if you can't get your votes out on Election Day, you will not win.

A.   Your Campaign Plan

That leads to our first point that we want to emphasize, and that is, make a **campaign plan**. As simple as this is, as logical as it is, many candidates find it hard to bring themselves to sit down with a paper and pencil or at their computer, and start answering questions such as, "What is my theme? What are the policies I stand for? What are the points and issues in this campaign? What does my opponent think about these issues?"

Other questions will be, "How will I raise the money to run my campaign? How will I get my message out through the media? How can I get volunteers to help me? How can I use the political structure of parties and interest groups to help my campaign?" *A plan is basically answering the questions that you ask yourself.* These are the questions that I will be covering with you also, but they're the questions that you need to answer for yourself when you draw up your campaign plan.

Here's my suggestion: Don't write a long campaign plan at first. Write a campaign plan that takes two or three pages to write or type. You may never want to show this original campaign plan to anybody else. But you should keep it in a place where you can read it regularly, and decide whether or not your plan is a good one, whether it's working, and whether you might want to show it to other people, either for them to critique it, and perhaps help you expand and improve it.

Or if you're doing some fund-raising, and the people that you're asking to help finance your campaigns say, "What are you doing to win the campaign?" your campaign plan is a ready answer that shows them you've done your part of the bargain, and you'd like their help in carrying it out.

Remember, a **Campaign Calendar** is an essential part of any campaign plan. But it is not sufficient by itself. I always suggest starting a calendar with Election Day and working backward to the present, since everything you do from now on in the entire campaign is aimed at Election Day. As we will see in subsequent discussion of many campaign aspects, the Calendar is a key component of your plan.

A campaign plan has many uses, and you can get as lengthy or as comprehensive as you want. But make sure that even if it is not elaborate, you start with a brief, concise, yet thoughtful, campaign plan with your personal imprint. If you're a Campaign Manager, the same planning applies to you. Every candidate, every Campaign Chairman, every Campaign Manager basically faces the same tasks.

B.   Your Campaign Organization

Organization. No matter what office in the entire nation you're running for, a plan with the same points will need to be considered, whether president or dogcatcher. The manager, the candidate, the chairman, all must be part of planning, and "sign off" on it. But you as the candidate have to work out the relationship between your plan and your organization. *Because a plan only works if it is brought*

7

to life by people implementing the plan. That's what organization is.

Here's my suggestion for setting up a campaign organization. As candidate, accept the fact that *you are going to be the person who cares the most about your campaign.* Others may help, hopefully, many others will help. And people will devote time and energy to your effort. But let's face it, you're the one whose reputation is on the line. You're the one who people will vote for or not vote for. Accept a strong active role in your own campaign. Be willing to take the advice of others, and be willing to delegate significant tasks to others, just as long as you remember, you are the one who's responsible.

When I run for office, I consider myself to be "chairman of the board." I'm not the "president, the managers or workers" who carry out the tasks of this temporary "company" we call a campaign. But I must be comfortable with every basic decision. When I get together with my campaign group, I don't want anyone who works with or for me to ever feel that if something goes wrong, I would say, "That's your fault." It's the candidate's responsibility. And don't be bashful to do a lot of work yourself. Sometimes candidates feel that others should be doing certain things because tasks are beneath their dignity. Don't feel like that. In a grass roots democracy, every activity that helps you win is important. And no matter how many volunteers, or how many people you can delegate to, you have to be willing, when needed, to do each task yourself, whether it's making phone calls, making lists, ringing doorbells, and every other job that goes into a winning campaign. That will help you understand what the people who are working for you are doing. And when they see you doing it, it reinforces their desire to redouble their efforts!

Well, so much for you, the candidate. Let's talk about other members of the organization. **Your key operative is your Campaign Manager.** This is someone that you appoint, that you trust, and who will commit himself or herself to working in a dedicated manner for your interests and your ultimate election. It's the Campaign Manager's job to tell you things you should do. Sometimes things that you might not want to hear. Sometimes the Campaign Manager really takes over the entire running of the campaign, with the support and encouragement of the candidate. And that's fine, as long as that sharing arrangement is understood. **Another key appointment is your Campaign Chairman or Chairwoman.** A Campaign Chairman need not be a worker in the same vein as a Campaign Manager. A Campaign Chairman is someone who will be the name on the letterhead. They will be someone who could sign letters or make press statements, or introduce you on special occasions. But this chair position is not necessarily someone who has all the time to devote that you would like, or that would be ideal, but yet it should be a person whose name and identity would be helpful to you in your neighborhood, your district or community. A Campaign Chairman is someone preferably who at a public meeting can say a few words, could introduce you, could make statements to the press in their name. It's also someone who could open doors for you, who possibly could help you with fund raising. It may be a long-time friend, it may be someone you met more recently, but who believes strongly in what you're doing. It could be someone already elected to office if in your locality that is an accepted practice. My suggestion is that someone who would be a good Campaign Chair would be active businessman or woman who may not be particularly active in politics, but who is respected in the community, and whose name is well-known. Sometimes a retired business leader might be available whom people remember and who also might have more time on their hands to actively help. Remember this, too, if there are other people that fit into your campaign, but for whom you can't think of the proper title, you can be inventive with your titles. For example, you can have an Honorary Chairman, or Honorary Co-Chairmen.

And of course, one essential person you'll need is a **Finance Chairman**. We'll talk about his or her responsibility more extensively later, under the fund raising topic. Remember in a typical campaign for local or state office, for the most part you're not going to be able to pay actual salaries to anyone, or at most one or a few people. It's far more important that you give people a title in this campaign that allows them to feel they are being recognized for their effort in your campaign, so don't be stingy with titles. A reminder, though, not to allow confusion to develop because of titles that you do give people. When you talk to them and ask them to sign on to your campaign, give them as clear a picture as you can of exactly what it is that you expect them to do. If it involves a lot of responsibility, don't try to make light of that. Don't try to recruit someone by minimizing the effort or time it would take. That's why with some people, you might want to say, "I don't need your time, but I would like to be able to use your name." With others, you might be able to say, "I'm going to need a lot of your time. I hope you believe in my candidacy, and that you'll do the job I'm asking you to do." Other positions in the campaign could be, depending on the kind of campaign you have, Campaign Coordinator,

Scheduler, Chairman for Volunteers, Election Day, Events, Public Relations and the Press, Canvassing, Telephoning. We'll be talking about these responsibilities as we go along. *Gauge the complexity and size of your organization according to your own campaign needs.*

C. Meetings

How many **meetings** should you have of your organization? I suggest you have two different kinds of organization meetings. First, your core group of five or six close-in people should probably meet once a week. Saturday morning is a common time but it could be an evening, a breakfast, or whatever suits the particular group you have assembled.

Core group meetings should be held from the beginning to the end of the campaign. Of course, if you have a spring primary in your state, a summer break is okay until about Labor Day, but in a close election meet as often as you and your group feel is necessary. Don't let these meetings drag on, or you'll lose the willingness of busy people to attend. Unfortunately, some people who are very helpful to a campaign are also very talkative, and it may tax your diplomacy. But you've got to give all your people the ability to talk without letting the talkative ones dominate at the expense of the others. Have a detailed agenda ready on one page, and whomever you choose to chair the meetings, pass out the agenda and stick to it, whether it's the candidate himself, the manager, or other authoritative member of your campaign. Move briskly through the agenda, and deal with each item.

Decide early whether you will use the meetings of this group as a decision-making group, an information-passing group, a sounding board for ideas, or a combination of these purposes. And then conduct the meetings accordingly. Don't let the meetings become a tug-of-war between competitive advisors. If that happens, restructure your meetings.

The other type of meeting which we might call "cheerleading" sessions, should be held perhaps twice or three times during the campaign period. These meetings, unlike the core group, smaller meeting of the first type, should be for all your workers to be invited, even if they can't come. And the tone of these meetings should be upbeat, positive and enthusiastic. You could call it a "rally." You and your major supporters, and perhaps special guests such as well-known and respected public officials, should speak delivering short, to the point, messages which add up to: your campaign is a winner! One such meeting should be held probably about six or seven weeks before the election, and another during the last two weeks as a kind of pre-election rally. Depending on social practices in your area, it could be a picnic, clam boil, or barbeque if the campaign can afford it or a supporter hosts it. Other times to consider this type of team-building meeting would be just before the election (say Friday evening if the election is on Tuesday which is customary) or at other times during an election cycle in which people might be feeling they don't know what's going on in the campaign, or there is a need to "re-charge" the troops.

D.   Strategy

Next, let's talk about **strategy**. What is strategy? ***Strategy is simply how you take your plan and put it to work.*** Remember this, like any general who goes into battle, you only have so many tanks, so many planes, so many soldiers, so much ammunition and support for your troops. How you *deploy all those resources* is your strategy, and you're just like that general. You have resources and you have an opponent. <u>There's a reason why both politics and war are tackled through something we call a campaign.</u> Estimate your strong points and your opponents. Discuss with your close campaign workers and advisors the biggest obstacles to success and the tools that you have to overcome them.

I think Americans like positive campaigns. They like a campaign in which you talk about your ideas and your experience and your qualifications. Then let the public decide, rather than just attack your opponent. But in many elections this isn't quite as easy as it sounds. We wouldn't have elections in the first place if our political system didn't expect disagreements!

As much as people may criticize "negative ads," they also, as any political consultant will readily tell you, read them intensely! Maybe this is akin to the tabloids people seem to buy in volume at the checkout counter. As any reporter will tell you, what people want to read about is *not* all the planes or trains that don't crash. Human nature tells us that it is what is unusual or involves conflict that gets our attention.

This is a very sensitive issue and one that you have to call on the basis of a lot of thought and consideration. You don't want "contrast" or "negative" campaigning to become an issue in itself which detracts from your basic positive message. It isn't always easy to decide, however, how to establish the way you will approach your opponent. If you are running against an incumbent, it is the most natural thing in the world for the election to be about whether he or she is doing a good job. Perhaps with some groups, you'll want to be more attacking if you need to present a clear contrast with your opponent (or opponents in a multi-candidate race). With other groups, you'll want to be more positive about yourself. Or balance the two aspects of what's wrong with the opponent and what's right with you.

Remember, there's nothing inherently wrong with so-called negative campaigning. Our whole system of democracy is based on having a contest of the opposing ideas and points of view so that people can choose. So don't feel badly about contrasting your views with your opponents. Or contrasting your experience, your qualifications, your knowledge of the community, your sensitivity with those of your opponent. Those are things that are quite fair to do. But do it in a positive vein. Do it in a way that doesn't seem to be based on attacking the opponent as a person; rather make it the ideas, the issues the policies that you are attacking. This is a little tricky and you may have to be careful how you do it. I think as with any other element of your campaign, we learn by doing, and you learn by getting out and talking to people, and finding out that something that comes across as too harsh should be dropped. Or on the other hand, that where you might be too hesitant or too soft, and where people aren't impressed, you need more vividness of contrast.

An example would be if you were running against an incumbent who has taken an unpopular action. Obviously, your strategy would be to attack. That doesn't mean a personal attack, but it does mean an attack on the decisions that led to this public controversy. Sometimes you may think that someone has taken an unpopular action, and yet find out there are many more than you originally thought who support it. So don't be too hasty in deciding to take one issue on which you think your opponent is vulnerable.

In many cases, especially if you're running against an opponent who is not well-known, or who does not have a public image, and whether they are an incumbent or not, and you're an incumbent or not, you may want to ignore that type of opponent. That's a different kind of a strategy from attacking, and we call it an *ignoring strategy rather than an attack strategy.* If your opponent is having a hard time getting known or being heard, don't do that favor for them!

If you are going to attack your opponent, make sure that any facts you use are absolutely correct. There's nothing that can undermine your credibility faster than a charge that you might make about an opponent that turns out to be factually incorrect. So make sure that you double-check especially those things you think sound particularly negative. ***Remember, don't hesitate to use negative information or arguments, which you judge appropriate, because they may well be used against you!***

Another part of strategy is **timing.** You have to figure out as part of your plan how much you want to do early in the campaign, how much you want to do in the middle of the campaign and how much will come in the closing stages. Your Campaign Calendar should reflect your judgment of pacing. When you're looking at a campaign from the very beginning, it may seem to you that the excitement needs to be built up early. But my suggestion is this. Remember, potential voters only begin to get involved in a campaign in the very closing stages. By the time you get to the closing stages, you may be physically and mentally exhausted. You may feel that you've done everything you can possibly do, just at the time when you need to go into the homestretch. So conserve yourself. Keep in mind the overall schedule you are following. Remember that most people are going to be keying into the race only at the tail end. And that's when you need to put on your "kick," as the racers call it, your final drive in the homestretch. You need to be physically and mentally prepared during the last three weeks of the campaign to give it all you've got, rather than to enter those last three weeks hoping the election will soon be over!

E.   Legal and Financial Requirements

So far we've been talking mostly about how to get elected. Let's make sure we don't bypass some of the important things we need to remember in a campaign: **legal issues and financial reporting.** When you anticipate running for office, these following issues are of critical importance. What is the filing date for the office that you seek? In other words, what is the latest date by which you must inform the official in charge of elections of your desire to be placed on the ballot? What requirements go along with it? For example, do you need to file a petition with a certain number of names on it? Must those names be obtained during a certain filing period? The dates of these periods can be given to you by your election official. Must you file in the name by which you are registered? In some states this may not matter. In other states, it might be very important. Take the attitude that requirements such as this must be met in their exact legal form by your campaign to avoid any challenge that might be made to your candidacy. In almost every state, there is a local or state election official who is responsible for certifying those who will be placed on the ballot.

Whether it is for a primary or for the general election, in making your statement of candidacy, you may have to fulfill other requirements, such as an affidavit concerning your citizenship, the length of time you have lived in the district, or possibly other qualifications for office. In most cases, these are minimal requirements that must be met, but none can be overlooked.

Another requirement to think about is the financial reporting of any expenses that you incur or for which you raise money as a candidate. We will talk later about raising money, but remember, in most states you can only accept money as a contribution towards your campaign after you have filed or legally established the committee and the committee name which can receive these monies. Again, every state has differences in exactly what details apply to filing. But almost every state requires you to establish your committee, to file it with the clerk or other official, and then to keep track of all the contributions and expenditures.

If yours is a race for which there is not much money required to be expended, it may be that in your state there is a provision for filing an affidavit that you have not spent more than a certain amount, or that you have spent it out of your own pocket. But be careful. Make sure that even if you get contributions or loans from others, even including family members, that you are meticulous in your bookkeeping. If your race is such that it takes a lot of bookkeeping, make sure that your volunteer treasurer can handle it, and think about having it done by someone who has been trained in accounting. Or if your campaign is big enough, and you have the money to spend, pay someone to do the bookkeeping. An investment of time and money into bookkeeping at an early stage can prevent a lot of heartache and headache later on. If your records are not properly kept, your deadlines for reporting are not met, remember, there is nothing that looks worse in the headlines than a candidate who either does not know the law, or who does not observe it. Even if it is just "carelessness" concerning financial reporting and accounting that led to it rather than any conscious desire to evade.

Legal counsel. In most races at the local level there are no major legal issues to be resolved, or lawsuits being filed against you or against your opponents. However, every candidacy, even a candidacy for the smallest township supervisor, still can have some of those sticky catches about what is and what is not legal. For example, whether or not a certain kind of expenditure, or a certain kind of a fund raising event, is proper. Or whether a certain person should be paid. Or whether it's within the law that regulates and governs campaign giving and spending. Or whether or not your papers have been filed properly. And it certainly doesn't hurt to have your papers reviewed, not only by your Campaign Manager, not only by yourself, but by someone who either knows the law as a lawyer, or someone who knows how to check and make sure that your legal papers are filed properly and in legal form. Moreover, if you're challenged during the campaign by an opponent, or by a member of the press as to a point of legality, it's good to know someone is standing by. Someone who will give you the benefit of their thinking, and who will be your advocate if a question comes up. I have found that often simply being able to refer problems to a respected attorney gives you a certain amount of credibility, if and when you choose to respond to questions. It also serves notice that you mean business about your campaign. Remember, you can get into a lot of fees if the lawyer you retained is doing it for pay. My suggestion is: approach a lawyer who is a friend, and who is willing to do this as a matter of public service. In most cases, you are not going to be taxing his time in any meaningful way. Of course, if that should develop, then you would want to make other arrangements.

A note on using formal benchmarks to build the campaign. Every time you file a legal paper in your campaign whether it be for filing a candidacy, to get on the ballot, stating your party registration, or whatever legal benchmark you meet, can be a great opportunity for public relations. For example, if in your state, you must qualify for the ballot by obtaining a certain number of signatures of other citizens, you can really go out and collect a lot of them and have the story be, not just that you filed, but that you more than exceeded the appropriate number of signatures. The more you can run up the number of people who have signed, the more impressive it may be. In addition, every person who signs a petition for you will have that little reinforcement in his mind when it comes to election day. It doesn't mean he will blindly vote for you, but it certainly means that he feels a stake in your candidacy. And you can build on that. One way you can build on it might be to correspond, because you have the address and the name of the person on the petition. At the early stage of the campaign this is one way you can recruit volunteers as well as thanking those who have taken the trouble to help you get your name on the ballot. Make sure that you read and meet all deadlines. In the heat of the campaign, often some of the simplest and most elementary steps may be overlooked by you or your workers if they are forgotten at key times. So take steps to make sure this doesn't happen to you.

We've already said that as part of the Campaign Plan that you should have the Campaign Calendar. The Campaign Calendar should be there for all to see as a reminder that certain activities or legal deadlines for certain requirements are approaching. In many states, there are financial reporting requirements, not only for the period following the election, but also in some cases prior to the election. When you review those dates, make sure that those who must meet the deadlines, such as the Campaign Treasurer or Manager know about them in addition to you. Then follow-up and make sure the deadlines are met.

Chapter Three

Resources For Your Campaign

**Money + Volunteers + Information +
Headquarters + Polling + Scheduling.**

Our next chapter covers resources you need for the campaign. Not only how to get these resources, but how to deploy them for your campaign.

A.   Money

Let's talk about **money**. In some ways, raising money is one of the areas that comes as a surprise to many candidates, even though we commonly accept the expenditure of dollars as a key component of our economic lives everyday for things on which we place value. You may think that having a finance committee and a finance chairman will put that responsibility on someone else. Well, it can't be. Look on it this way. *People who give money in politics are, in some ways, like people who vote. They want to know why they should do it.* Giving money really helps win other votes. And so, maybe, someone doesn't have a lot of time to volunteer for your campaign. But on the other hand, would like to help you financially. Take advantage of them. They feel they have an *investment* in you the product, you the candidate. If you believe strongly in yourself, your goals, your policies, your aspirations to help people, then people whom you approach to donate will feel that. Sometimes, they'll want to give you money without you even asking, but don't count on that too often. We all like to be asked. And don't make the mistake of thinking that only rich people can contribute money in politics. Yes, they are the people who can make large contributions, maybe that you and I couldn't make. And hopefully, you'll get your share of such large contributions. But running for public office is just as important to our society as many other causes that people willingly donate to. Little League, church, or a favorite charity. No gift is too small. And the persons who give once may well give again, if they feel they've made a wise investment in you.

People including the press love to complain about the "high costs" of campaigning. You might hear this in your discussions with potential contributors. Your own particular race may not cost more than the value of getting some signs and brochures printed. Maybe the cost of your race is nominal. But these days even candidates for local and state offices can end up spending significant dollars. Actually since the costs of campaigning are almost entirely spent on getting your name and message out to others, it is hard to criticize candidates for doing what any "product" does in our society, namely paying the going rates for communicating. If newspaper, radio or television advertising rates were not what they are, campaign costs would be a lot less. (Press: take note!) The amount spent on political campaigns, if we add them all up, might sound large...until we compared those costs with the promotion amount spent for the costs of automobile, insurance and soap advertising! Our democracy functions on communication just like our economy.

Here's what I suggest to get started raising the funds you will need. When you first start your campaign, make up a letter. Consider it a letter to a personal friend. And send it to the list of 30, 40, as many people as you can who are your friends, neighbors and associates. Close enough friends that you don't mind asking them for money. And, basically, say to them, "I've made the decision to run for mayor," or whatever the office is. "I need your help. Our town and its leadership are important questions for you. And you can be a part of my race by allowing me to get my message out to the community. I would deeply appreciate your support." Now, you can add a lot to that basic letter. But that's the message you want to convey. Put in the issues that you feel strongly about. Put in the letter the issues that people may have on their minds. But don't make it too lengthy and don't be defensive. Above all, be positive about yourself.

Next, mail to various groups which you belong to or with which you are familiar. And you may want to include return envelopes. Increasingly email and social media are used to convey the same messages traditionally sent in letters so don't hesitate to use that form of communication for fund raising as well. Your website should include a prominent "click here to contribute" feature.

Have **events** to raise money. People often are happy to contribute to your campaign by buying tickets for events, a reception, a dinner, a breakfast, a dance. Whatever is appropriate in your community. Don't ask too much, but also don't ask too little, either. Some events you'll want to do for their political value, in other words to get a lot of potential voters there even if the ticket price is low and raising some money is a side benefit. A $25 ticket to a picnic will probably end up paying for not much more than the event itself, but it will give people a sense of commitment as well as fun. Enthusiasm manifests itself in both ways, attendance and contribution. (Sometimes you might put on events that cost nothing to attract people to the campaign... but they will become potential financial supporters.) But do have some specifically targeted fundraising events at several levels. Ranging, perhaps, from a 10, 15 or 25-dollar spaghetti dinner, or whatever is popular in your area, to the hundred dollars or so reception or dinner for local business leaders. Remember it may be the social event that triggers the contribution, because it is a specific date, a specific time and a specific location. But people know and understand the real reason is to make a financial contribution. Not the cost of the food or drink or entertainment.

Personal visits are a good way to approach people. Take a friend or your manager, or go by yourself if you like. And visit people in their own offices to ask for contributions. Pitch your suggested contribution to what you think they may be able to contribute. There is no substitute for face-to-face fund raising. Your finance chairman is in charge of putting the budget together, planning how to raise the funds, and either asking himself or engaging others, for potential contributors to give money. And he should have a plan, just as you have an overall campaign plan, that has targeted amounts and the dates by which you hope to achieve that level of funding. The finance chairman should have a finance committee, other members that the chairman or you recruit to help you raise money. And together, they may want to do planning for the amounts that each will take the responsibility for. Expenditures should be identified early on the basis of estimates and information, should be done in conformance to the overall campaign plan, and should be monitored constantly by the finance chair and the person we discuss next.

Also, remember an important position in finance is your campaign **treasurer**. The one who receives the checks when they are written, and who writes checks for your expenditures. And who reminds you to write thank you notes when you receive contributions. Often your state campaign laws may give the treasurer certain legal responsibilities so make sure the person who volunteers for this task understands the serious nature of undertaking it.

B.   Volunteers

Volunteers. Once you've established your organization, you'll need to start thinking about the other people who will be necessary to win, the additional volunteers to fulfill all the campaign functions. Undoubtedly, when you get into a campaign, and your family, friends and acquaintances know about it, they will begin to say things to you. Like, "Let me know if I can help." Be ready for these volunteers. Take down their names and phone numbers. Have candidate business cards that you carry with you, that have your name, address, phone number, business phone, email. Hand them out liberally and ask those to whom you give them to contact the campaign. Remember this. **Politics is lists, lists and more lists.** It may be a list of voters that you wish to reach.

But to reach these voters, you'll need a list of volunteers. Another list, of course, would be people who have given to your campaign financial contributions. Or a list of those who may give to your campaign in the future, your prospects. I'm going to talk more about volunteers in a minute. But let me just make a point now about lists. Keeping your lists up to date can be a real headache. Maybe you know someone who is very organized and who likes to keep lists, and who loves to work on their own home computer. In that case, put them to use making, keeping and managing your lists.

Let's talk specifically about the volunteers list. You can start by taking your own telephone pad that you have in your home or office, or that you keep digitally, and go through it. Asking yourself as you look at each name, will this person help my campaign? Could I call him or her and ask them? Take your church directory, your Rotary Club roster, the Little League coaches that you've worked with. Directories of people in your profession whom you may know, or who might like to know someone in their group who is running for office, even if you don't know them that well. What do you use a volunteer's list for? Well, tasks are numerous in a campaign. Here are some of the things that you might be asking volunteers to do. Host a coffee or reception in their home so that you can meet their neighbors. You could ask them to put up a sign in their yard, if you live in an area in which yard signs are used for your campaign. And we'll talk some more later about other methods of getting your message out in a similar vein. Ask your volunteers to put a bumper sticker on their car. Many people don't like to put bumper stickers on their car. But there are many who, because they like you, will be willing to do it. But you'll probably have to ask.

Get someone to read the newspapers for you, all the news-papers in the area that you want to run in. Maybe there's only one. Maybe there are several. This is a good job for a volunteer in the district that you're interested in, if you're running for the legislature. Or the town that you live in may have daily newspapers and weekly newspapers. Ask someone who likes to read, and who probably reads them anyway. Maybe, someone who's at home a good deal of the time and could do this along with other things. Or someone who simply likes to read newspapers. And who will let you know every time there is an article about you, your opponent, or any issue that is involved in your race.

One of the most important things you can ask volunteers to do is to work for you on Election Day. We're going to talk about Election Day later on in some detail. Because as I've said before, Election Day is the day when you can convert all your sales into votes. You can't do it alone. You'll need lots of help from other people. Maybe volunteers could help go around to neighbors that you might not be able to cover yourself, if you have a large area to cover. The volunteer would knock on the door and say, "I'm working for John Smith. Can I give you a piece of literature? And we'd like you to vote for him on Election Day." This is called "canvassing" and we'll discuss it later, also.

A volunteer to help organize the volunteers is always a good idea. They can help you get people slotted into tasks. You're likely to find that not everyone who seems to want to work on your campaign will actually be available when you have a task. Maybe you'd like to get a mailing out to the voters in your district. And once you have your voters list from the courthouse or city hall, or from your political party headquarters, you'd like some volunteers to help you make that mailing. Putting the stamps on, sealing the envelopes, stuffing the letters into the envelopes. Chances are you can start out with your list of volunteers and find that many people, although they might be willing to do some of these things, don't have time or don't like to do other things. So one of the things that you need to do first is to match, on your volunteer list, the names of those volunteers with the various tasks that you need.

If you need volunteers who are good at one thing, often, they will be a base of volunteers to do something else. For example, suppose you're going to do telephoning prior to the election to advocate support for you or your candidate, as we'll discuss under phone banks. If you start down the list of volunteers and ask, you'll find some people don't like to phone. Some people won't have the time to phone. Maybe, you have to urge some people to help you. So do it this way. Give them a specific number of hours and don't make it to onerous. For, say, two hours of phoning at a time when it might be convenient for them. When we talk about telephoning later, we'll discuss exactly how to do this.

But while we're talking about volunteers, let's just make a note of the fact that normally you'll be wanting them to help you from about 5:00 p.m. to 8:00 p.m. Those are the hours in which you'll find most people home, or available to volunteer for that matter, in today's world. So whether you're canvassing or making phone calls, if when you recruit your volunteers, you can say, "Could you come in from 6:00 to 8:00 on Thursday?" That has a lot more specificity to it than just saying, "Can you help me on my phone bank?" Or "Will you help me as a volunteer?" It's like anything else in life, often a few people do most of the work. And many more people will do something to help, but cannot help carry the "heavy lifting" that you and your few highly motivated campaign workers will probably end up doing. Many homemakers, retirees or those with flexible work schedules may be able to help during the day too.

While I'm on the subject of volunteers, I'd like to make a comment that may be helpful to you. It's your job, as the candidate, to motivate your volunteers. The motivation may be sparked in their own minds. But you, as the candidate or the campaign chairman or manager, need to constantly reinforce those who are working. By letting them know what your campaign is all about, what your themes are, why it's important that they help you to accomplish your goals. The more they understand the big picture, even if they are doing routine or seemingly insignificant tasks, the more they will feel their work is valuable and appreciated. And thank them. Gratitude goes a long way in our democracy where volunteers are so important to any candidate's campaign. **Thank them. Thank them. Thank them again.**

C.   Information

Information. In today's society, knowledge is power. Make sure you or a campaign worker, possibly a research director, if you want them to have a title, have in one place, or at least have access to, the publications about your jurisdiction. Annual reports, budgets, newspaper articles and other official or unofficial sources of information. Visit your local library and spend some time. You'll be surprised how much you can gain in the way of information. Websites may offer information as well such as minutes of past meetings, and other documents about the policies your campaign is based on or which you are expected to know.

You may want to use this information to develop **issue papers** to distribute, which are brief, but well thought out statements about your positions. As a campaign progresses, sometimes issues change, depending on different circumstances or your opponents' positions. So keep abreast, especially if knowing what's in the news will help show your mastery of the issues. Also, make sure you do what is called **opposition research.** Check out the literature and statements made by your opponents or statements made by them in the press. Verify the facts and claims they make for accuracy and consistency. And, of course, remember an opponent's campaign will be doing the same thing about you. I'm not talking here about "digging up dirt" on opponents which perhaps some of your enthusiastic supporters may be urging. That to me is not an activity worthy of your campaign…but again be aware your opponents may not have your scruples.

Before every appearance, speech or interview, prepare yourself. Be briefed by your manager or another worker, and perhaps a knowledgeable person or people who know in depth the issues about which you may be asked. To review what you will be saying to test and perhaps question your facts and arguments as an interviewer might. Be alert for articles that help broaden your knowledge and collect them in your research files.

D. Headquarters

Headquarters. A recurring question in campaigns, especially smaller campaigns in towns or townships, is "Should I have a headquarters?" Let me talk about the pros and cons. You have to make up your own mind. And like so many of these questions, there is no one right answer. In a campaign in a small town, where much of the campaigning is personal, it may make very little difference whether or not you have a campaign headquarters. You do need to have your records somewhere. You probably need to have a telephone at which people can call you. For these you may want to use your home. There's nothing wrong with using your home as a headquarters, but it does mean certain things. Volunteers may enjoy being at your home, but may not feel as comfortable if they are not your personal friends. Perhaps, you have a very good home situation, where people can come into your home and do the volunteer work that they would be doing on a campaign, without feeling or actually intruding on your personal life.

But if you are going to have large mailings, if you are going to have a phone bank with phones, if you are going to have a lot of meetings, or need a place to store information or bulky campaign paraphernalia, you should think about having a headquarters. And if you want to have a visible presence, say, on the main street of your town, then you need a headquarters.

The best way I have found to get a headquarters is to ask a business friend of yours who has real estate if he or she happens to have any vacant storefronts. Many times it is to the advantage of building owners to have someone

31

occupying space for insurance purposes. Insurance is usually cheaper if someone is on the premises. So it may be
to their advantage to have a campaign headquarters in
an empty building. Remember, if in your state, such a use
is a campaign contribution, just make sure it's reported.
Another way to handle it is to pay rent. Often, the rent
can be very nominal, because the landlord wants to have
someone in the building. Of course, the building doesn't have
to be fancy. If you are going to have people working in there,
then you need restroom facilities, and parking space may be
a problem. So it's always good to find a headquarters that
has parking for volunteers that you may need to work in
your headquarters. This, sometimes, is made more difficult
by the other use of the headquarters. Which is to have a big
window on Main Street with a big sign that says, "Smith for
County Commissioner," or whatever office you are running
for. Sometimes the buildings on main streets are the ones
that don't have the parking. You will have to balance this
all out in your mind.

My suggestion would also be to have the headquarters,
if you have one, close to your home. It makes a lot more
convenience for you and your family members to run back
and forth, and it saves you time. One thing a headquarters
does is to give a campaign a certain amount of legitimacy.
It makes it seem like a real campaign if there's a place
that has an identity associated with your name and your
aspirations. It gives people a place to look at, as they pass
by. And it reinforces your name identity. It gives people a
place to call if they have questions. Of course, they could also
do these things by calling your home or your place of business. My suggestion would be to be very careful, however,
in terms of using your business. In the first place, it might

be, technically, a campaign contribution to yourself, which normally is perfectly legal. But in many places, it must be reported. And in some places, it might not even be legally feasible. This is something you should check out or talk to your legal counsel about, as we discussed previously in Legal and Financial Requirements in Chapter Two. It's inevitable that a certain number of phone calls and correspondence or people dropping by a business place will be political. And if you're engaged in a political race, there's nothing wrong with that. It's a part of the normal human and personal communication. But to the extent that it involves using equipment, machinery, supplies, et cetera, I'd suggest being careful. If you do use your own business supplies, then, make sure that the transactions that you conduct are done according to the campaign law.

Headquarters as an example of how to relate activity to the legal context. This may all sound a bit complicated for a simple political race for a local or state office. But my feeling would be you can't be too careful with this kind of thing. Even if it seems somewhat time consuming and even cumbersome to do these things, it's always better to do more than is necessary than not do enough. Interestingly enough, and it's a shame really, the press and the public seem to expect that regular people like you and I, when we enter politics, suddenly become exposed to the idea that any one small error in bookkeeping can be magnified. An opponent can take an error and blow it out of proportion. But you can't blame the press which has the task of covering all the aspects of a campaign. But sometimes what the press is doing is picking up their cues from your opponent. So although it may sound slightly paranoid, remember the old saying-- it's humorous, but it has an element of truth-- **"Just**

because you're paranoid doesn't mean they're not out to get you." In other words, people are going to be looking at you very closely. Maybe some people whom you may not even know, who have no particular reason to be against you personally. But they might find that politically it is in their interest to embarrass you or expose a mistake that you make. Or to take something you have done that is not a mistake and may not be an error or illegal. And yet, try to make it sound that way. I hate to say it, but politics has an element to it that is not always showing the best side of human nature. It comes from competition and a desire to win, which are perfectly natural human instincts. But may not always lead us, as human beings, to portray ourselves in the best light.

Back to discussing the Headquarters as a resource, one problem with headquarters is that you may end up putting so much work into organizing and manning a headquarters that you are draining away valuable volunteer efforts that should be going somewhere else. Campaign headquarters can be lonely places, and often you might think that people would want to come to a headquarters to find out about your candidate. But then, you might find that you'll get a usual amount of casual drifters and kids instead of actual voter prospects. And, of course some serious citizens, as well, may come to the headquarters. You'll have to judge this for yourself.

You don't want one or more volunteers sitting for long periods of time in a headquarters, waiting for people who don't come. On the other hand, if the reason for your manning the head-quarters in the first place is to accomplish volunteer tasks, then, that is something that will be valuable, whether or not inquiring people do visit the headquarters. Remember, the visibility value is there, whether or not anybody stops in. People see the headquarters. And if you're also using it to get volunteer work done, such as addressing mail, then, that may be a good way to combine those goals of visibility and task accomplishment.

E. Polling and Targeting

Polling and targeting. What about political polling? It seems every time we read about politics, we see a reference to polling. Usually in the bigger races, polling is important, but it's also expensive. I am sure you might like to know some of the things that polling could tell you. For example, how well do people know me? If you took all of the people who are likely to vote on Election Day and ask them, "Do you know Jane Smith?" What percentage would you get? I think many people, even people who have been in public life a long time, would be very disappointed to know just how few people really identify their names or the offices they hold. (Much less, what those offices actually do!) Of course, it isn't just how many people know you. It's also the kind of thought they have about you. In other words, are they favorable or unfavorable? There are some people who have very high ratings of identification, but who also might get very high negative ratings.

Chances are, in most races for local office, the professionally conducted poll that would cover these questions is too expensive for you. A poll usually costs four or five thousand dollars, even for a small one, when done professionally. But there are some ways that you can have what amounts to a poll done by your volunteers, saving the money and advancing your campaign. Almost any time you hear from a lot of people about how you are doing, you can say in a rough, perhaps amateurish way, that is a poll. An example would be when you are conducting a volunteer phone campaign, which as the calls are made detects widely held points of view. Hearing from groups what they think by attending their meetings, or receiving communications in any systematic way, gives you feedback that is comparable to an actual poll. And it may tell you, more importantly, what you need to know for your race.

There is a big difference between a volunteer conducted listening post and a professional poll. And you shouldn't assume that there is an exact equivalence between them. But you can get the benefit of each kind as long as you understand what the results mean to you. Since you want to be in politics, you need to develop a keen eye and ear for what people are thinking and feeling, by putting lots of random sources of opinion into a pattern in your brain.

An important basic resource is the **analysis that you do of past election results**, which is called targeting. Don't make this more complicated than it needs to be. But make sure you get all the data you can about past elections in your jurisdiction from your library, courthouse or city hall, or as is growing more common, the local elections office website. Using that information, comparing it to your race, will help you make predictions about where, what precincts or what towns, you can do the best in, so that you can concentrate on those areas for your campaign. For this, you may want some advice from your "kitchen cabinet" of advisors and workers. This **targeting** process will help your allocation of time in the campaign. And time is one thing that you can't make any more of.

We discuss targeting in more detail in the Grassroots Campaigning chapter.

F. Scheduling

Speaking of time, let's discuss **scheduling**, how to use your time most efficiently. There's an old saying among political people, *"the schedule drives the campaign,"* and it's true!

Someone needs to have the specific responsibility for scheduling in your campaign. You may be able to do this yourself. Remember your proactive responsibilities however. Probably there will be so much in the way of phone calls and correspondence revolving around scheduling, it usually shouldn't be you. However, you must be in regular communication with the scheduler. The scheduler should also constantly consult the Campaign Calendar which is part of the Campaign Plan discussed in Chapter Two and work with the Campaign Manager in making sure the candidate and the whole campaign is not only using time wisely day to day, but that the day to day activities properly reflect the strategic timing of the original plan.

Here are a few tips. When scheduling, don't overdo it. Don't stretch yourself too thin in the effort to cover too many appearances in one period of time. Allow yourself time for transportation. Allow yourself a little cushion to gain some rest or thinking time when you may need it. Also, make sure that your scheduler gets complete directions with the names and phone numbers of the places where you are going. This should not be difficult in these days of mapquest and GPS.

If you can do this, print the schedule. Don't over-circulate the schedule. But make sure that your family members, your close workers and your campaign manager know where you are going to be. As simple as this sounds, some campaigns don't have good internal communication. And it leads to problems. Try to put regular practices of information and schedule sharing into your campaign routines.

Also, in scheduling, I guess it just common sense to advise bunching events or appearances in places convenient in location to each other that will minimize the time in between.

Make sure that you keep your **overall goals** in mind when you schedule. In other words, make appearances that bolster the themes and issues that you have identified as being important. And don't just do "re-active" scheduling, responding only to invitations that come to you. Do "pro-active" scheduling, seeking out and if necessary creating the events that you want and need to convey your message and reach the groups that are part of the campaign plan.

Sometimes, you'll have to make a decision between conflicting events. This is the toughest challenge of scheduling. But a few tips here would be to tend to give priority to where there are media, television and other press. Rather than going to where there may be larger numbers, go to where the "multiplication factor" will help you end up reaching the greatest number. Especially, go to where you can convince new friends and supporters, rather than to those who may already be in your camp. This at first may seem to go against the grain, since you know and feel close to your friends and supporters, but remember they will be for you already and should understand your need to reach the prospects rather than themselves.

If, inevitably, you do find that you have a conflict between two desirable events, first try to resolve it by going to events for shorter periods of time at each event, but going to all of them. If you have to skip one, send a "high ranking" representative such as your campaign chairman, campaign manager, or perhaps, a spouse or family member.

Also, be careful of making commitments before you are ready to decide that an appearance is in your best interest. It may frustrate the person who is asking for your time. But it's better to have them wait until you are sure you can keep the commitment, than to end up making more commitments than you can keep.

Chapter Four

Communicating Your Message

Advertising + Public Relations + Press + Internet

Now we're ready to talk about the key topic of your **campaign communications**: how to create your message and how to communicate it through advertising, public relations, the press, and through the internet. The first part of this section is advertising. Advertising is the form of communications that <u>you control yourself</u>. The next part is public relations. That's what's <u>written about you or communicated about you by others</u>. Then we'll look at how to deal with the <u>press</u>. And finally we'll talk about the <u>electronic media</u>, how you can use the forms of electronic media, social networking, blogging and e-mail, to help your campaign communicate your message.

A.   Advertising

First let's talk about **advertising**. It includes a lot of the strategy and themes that will go into your campaign, and a lot of the materials which will be discussed later in this program. This is an important section of this book because you control the content of advertising and it is your main direct method of communicating the message the way you want it!

"How to best spend your money?" is a key advertising question. Advertising is everything from a button, a poster, a bumper sticker, an ad in the paper, an ad on the radio or television, whether cable or broadcast. The most expensive advertising in almost any campaign is probably going to be from broadcast television, whether in a major media market or even in smaller market areas. In a relative sense, even in a small media market, or a smaller station, you may still pay relatively high rates compared to other forms of advertising.

My advice is to spend some time at the very beginning of the campaign with your financial advisors and your media advisors, thinking about the questions which will apply to almost everything that you publish, print, or otherwise use in advertising. Here are some of the things I think you should determine rather quickly once you have made up your mind to run, and you are ready to start communicating your message.

The first decision you should make early is your **theme**. By theme here, I don't mean a deep philosophical idea, as much as I mean a catchy phrase, a slogan that you can apply to hopefully all of your literature. This may be something unique to your campaign such as balancing the budget, or defending the right to have zoning, but I'd caution against slogans that are too specific to issues, unless it is an overriding aspect of the campaign. I know it sounds self-serving but here's where you have to try to convey your attitude, your ideas, and your thoughts for goals that you would like to have your jurisdiction accomplish. There are lots of old clichés that we can find in use when it comes to a slogan but some of them may be quite useful such as "Committed and Caring," or "Caring and Committed," "Experienced," "Proven," "Leadership," "Wants the best for this town's government." I say don't put too many words here, but something that people will remember, and even if you want to list some of your attributes, pick the leading characteristics that you want to be known by. Don't feel you have to overwhelm the reader of your brochure, or your ad copy, with every last good thing that can be said about you. Very few other people have the desire to read that.

Next a seemingly minor question, but I would argue an important one, what are your **campaign colors**? So much of communications is visual, even when we are resorting to words that we want people to remember, that we need to think of the impact of the context in which the words are presented. This applies to brochures, signs, electronic advertising, websites, you name it. You don't have to use the same colors on everything, but I would strongly suggest that you think about consistency of identity. You want people to see a certain symbol, certain colors and to associate them with you in your campaign.

Don't try to be like everybody else, but yes red, white, and blue are probably the favorite colors for politicians and they have a strong positive impact if used correctly. However you should pick colors that you think fit you, and your theme and your personality. There are certain color combinations that are fairly traditional; blue and white, blue and gold, and other combinations that are less usual, but may still be striking, such as blue and green, or yellow and black.

Experiment; have friends react to your ideas. You can get from a local printer booklets or pamphlets that may give you some color ideas, and any printer also has a register of colors which allows you to look at colors by themselves and in combination. If you have any doubts about it, ask your printer to do some sample printing that may not commit you forever to the colors, but a flyer or a handout that incorporates certain ideas so that you can see them, how they look and how others react.

Let's discuss a few of the pluses and minuses for the <u>media that you may use in advertising</u>; first newspapers, then television and radio.

Newspapers are avidly read by a certain portion of the population, and perhaps the best way to reach these readers is through explicit ads in newspapers. You control (and pay for) the entire content. If your local newspaper doesn't charge very much, you can probably advertise regularly during the final period of the campaign, whether it's a weekly or a daily. If it's a weekly, remember you have to begin planning about a month ahead of the election to properly stagger the appearance of your ads in that newspaper. Most weekly newspapers publish toward the end of the week, and so that means that the last chance that you may have would be in the edition that comes out in the week prior to the election.

Some people believe in placing small ads that appear regularly in certain places such as the classifieds, sports, or editorial area of the newspaper, even before the closing period of the campaign. Different newspapers have different practices, but you should know yours and then choose the most effective area of the newspaper if the newspaper will let you choose. Sometimes you may have to pay a special premium to get into the position that you want.

My perspective on newspaper advertising. I do not believe in going heavily into newspaper advertising. You do have to do it to some extent, partly because your supporters will be looking for it, and partly because for some people it may be the only way they will see your ads. I'm more inclined to use radio and television where it is possible, because they are more vivid to the person receiving and also are heard without the person having to be motivated to pick up a newspaper and read your article. I also prefer "direct mail," the use of the post office to deliver your message to large numbers of people, since we know everyone at least looks at their mail and even if they say they don't like all the political junk mail they may receive at the time of an election, they do read the attractive and well produced pieces...at least long enough to get your name and theme even if they then trash it. I'll cover mailings later on in more detail.

In many smaller races **television** is not going to be an option that you have, especially if you live in a large metropolitan area where the cost of broadcast television advertising is very high. You *will* have the opportunity to go on cable television in your own area, at better rates and with more ability to target to smaller areas. That is a growing type of medium that I think is readily adapted to the candidate in the smaller scale race. I have used it at the local level and it doesn't cost too much. You can probably reach, on any particular cable system, a relatively small slice of the total viewership. And if you can identify a local station that is used a lot, or put an ad on the so-called bulletin board type cable channel scheduling the time or the weather appears and many people tune in solely for those items, you will have made a very good buy, as the media professionals say. You can also use 30 second spots on cable or on broadcast television. They are relatively inexpensive to make, but be advised if you are going to go into television chances are you will need approximately $5,000 as a minimum or you will not be able to cover professional production costs for the ads that you will have. Also remember that media professionals advise that spots on radio or television, even if professionally done and seemingly effective, are not *really* effective unless shown with a lot of "redundancy" which means airing them a lot!

Radio is the best way to advertise in many smaller elections. People listen to radio on the way to work, on the way home from work, and in many cases while they are getting up in the morning or at other predictable times. So you can, with a wise use of what you know about people's listening habits, reach a large number of people with a more vivid impression than is left by the printed word. I am not in favor of longer than 30 second spots on either television or radio. To me a 30 second radio spot can be very effective. It can be read by you, or you may use the talent available at the local station. I have sometimes in the past specified a particular broadcaster as the voice "talent" who is well known on the local radio station, because he's been there so long and has a listener following. But there are many announcers available at a station who will do it simply as part of their duty once you have paid for the ad. If you want to get a little fancier, in addition to having voices, and you want to have music, the station itself will probably help you produce the ads. If you have bought some significant number of ads from the station, they will view it as something which they would do to help you as they would for any paying client. They may

45

be able to get you some ideas as to how to format your ad, what type of introduction to use, and the approach that you will want to apply in your ad.

When you are planning your media campaign, don't hesitate to talk to the advertising or program managers of stations or the editors of newspapers. Particularly if you approach them from the point of view of needing their expertise and valuing their advice and you will be able to get a lot of help in that manner, especially since they look forward to your placing many ads with them. If you are running within a part of a political organization and have access to people who have been involved with campaigns before, there's probably no better way to design your own ideas than by getting as much advice as you can from those who have been through this process.

One point I would like to make is that if you live in a community where everyone in the media knows you, and each other, this may call for some careful thought. If you decide to advertise in one newspaper rather than another, then you may irritate another newspaper and the same goes with radio and television stations. You should know that they watch each other very carefully to see whether advertisers use one more than another, or exclusively. If that is your situation I'd say don't try to create that kind of ill will. You should probably make sure that if you advertise on one station, you also advertise on another. I have been put in the position in the past where between a larger station and a smaller station of using the same ad, but just placing it more often on the station that reaches larger numbers of people.

In this next discussion I'm going to be talking about election materials, the things that you will use to briefly state your name, your office, your message and do this in forms that will allow you and your message to reach and be remembered by as many people as possible. This is a very important section under advertising. If I asked you how you saw the names of most people who are running for office, you might reply, in addition to the advertising we've already discussed, "Posters, bumper stickers, signs on poles, billboards, and political buttons." Studies have shown that different people get their political "cues," that is, their ideas about whom they will vote for and what issues are important, from many different sources.

Not every medium you use is going to be equally effective with all groups of people, and that's why, just as the general uses a combination of air cover, artillery and infantry, we are going to use different forms of advertising materials to reach different, and in many cases the same, audiences.

There's no particular order so let's just start with some of the items that you will want to consider using in your campaign. In the first place remember in all your materials use the same colors and the same theme as we've already discussed and the same lettering and print style. You can work that out with your printer. Obviously it takes a lot of effort to achieve consistency, but if you are dealing with just one printer it makes it a lot easier. Don't choose the printer lightly. Unless you happen to have someone who is offering you a good discount, or you have a long-time friend whom you feel must have the business, make it competitive. You might want to conduct bids. In other words, outline everything you think you will have printed. It doesn't have to be exact. Make the list and give it to two or three printers and ask them to go through it with you, and then to come up with the best cost as to what price they can give you. Sometimes if they have a chance to do more printing items, they will give you a break on each individual item. Sometimes they won't and you'll find printers even who don't want to do business at all with political candidates because they've had a few bad experiences in the past. Don't be surprised when you order printing or perhaps other services that the business person may ask you to put up a deposit or to pay in advance.

Let's proceed with the things that we want to have printed. In the first place you'll want to have posters and possibly posters of different sizes to accomplish different goals. One thing you want to have posters for, remembering our principle of the importance of Election Day, is posters for the critical period: election day itself. Even though it may seem far away in the campaign at this point, remember it is the ultimate objective of all your campaign activities. So it doesn't hurt to think about the kind of posters you will want on Election Day and how many to order that you can stock away for that time. In your area there may be an opportunity to put up posters on a telephone pole near the polling place or on a garage door or on a wall, so it means you have to figure three to five posters for each polling place in your district or your town.

You could also use these same signs throughout the campaign in peoples' yards, especially if they're on heavier stock of paper to withstand the weather. The poster may be identical with the one that you use on Election Day or for that matter throughout the campaign. Remember, the most important thing about posters is people need to know your name. It is satisfying to see a picture on the poster. I've had this experience, and it struck me at first as strange to see my face looking down at me from a sign. But it's more important to keep in mind that you do not vote for pictures in the ballot booth, you vote for a name. The whole point is if you have a picture, make it an attractive picture that leads the viewer of the sign to remember the name. The name must be in large, easy to read print. Mainly the last name is important because that's what will be the thing to key the person's memory when they go into the voting booth. I'm not opposed to have a first name there also, but my suggestion would be put the first name in smaller print and make the one vivid name to be remembered from your poster your last name. Some people running for office are known by nicknames and if that is the case, and that is the image of friendliness and familiarity you want to project, that should be highlighted.

It may be that people need to be reminded also of the office for which you are running, but remember when they get into the voting booth the names that they see there will be associated with offices on the ballot. They don't have to remember what you're running for as much as they do have to remember...yes, your name!

One way of doing it is to put a picture at the top with perhaps the word, "Elect," or "Re-Elect," and then have the name "John" in smaller print, "Smith" in large print, and then again at the bottom the office for which you are running such as County Commissioner, Town Council, Township Supervisor and so forth.

In the past, sign construction was fairly simple. Printed cardboard signs would be stapled on stakes for yard signs, or tacked or stapled on poles, fences and so forth. Today these cardboard signs still find plenty of use, but the prevailing practice is to have printed plastic "slipovers" on upside-down U shaped metal brackets. These are less expensive to produce, stand up to the weather and easier to put up and take down. Your political candidate's catalog of items to order will tell you how to place the order and when to expect to receive them. With websites and email to speed the process you will have your name all over town before you know it.

You will have to know the practices (and sometimes laws) in your area that affect putting up yard signs and public signs. Yard signs are easier to the extent they are on people's property who have made the decision to have them there. But when visible public space near roads, railroad or transit stations, or median strips, is used you are taking it on yourself to post your signs and often those who own such property...including the local utilities who own poles or the department of transportation...don't particularly like political signs. Although purists might say there is some sort of First Amendment right to put up political signs, I think that's pressing the point. If owners don't want the signs they can take them down and if that is the case you have to decide how energetic to be in replacing them.

Don't get your signs out either too early or too late. That may sound easy advice to follow, but as in many competitive advertising campaigns, watching the competition is important. If suddenly a month before the election the opponent's signs begin to appear, you may have planned to put them up three weeks out, but now have to decide whether to match the opposition activity. But maybe a month is too soon, and the signs will disappear or deteriorate long before the election. Maybe three weeks is better. The idea is to get them up perhaps just before the average voter begins to be aware there is an election taking place, and thus 2-3 weeks could be about right. Ten days before the election would be the latest you would want to get them up. If everyone puts their signs in the same places, the impact of each sign is diminished. Go for a multiplicity of yard signs, and also for those hard to reach but highly visible spots.

If the signs that you have prepared for the campaign and the election (remember to conserve the number you will eventually need on Election Day) are for outside use and as yard signs, they are probably large such as 20" by 30." Then you might also want to have some smaller posters made, replicas of the larger, that you can use inside if you're having events in church basements, union halls or even people's homes for which larger posters may not be suitable.

One thing to try to do is every time you are going to appear or speak anywhere, have someone in the role that one of my best campaign managers used to call a **front runner**. Their job is to go in advance before you arrive, and make sure that your posters are up, your brochures are out and that in general the place you are going to shows you off to best advantage. Remind people who you are and try to leave a lasting memory with them. That's why materials such as a poster help you do that.

In fact, if you have posters in your car, when your picture is taken either by newspapers or for other types of promotion, it doesn't hurt to have a poster or bumper sticker in your hand or behind you, so that in the picture it vividly imprints your name with your face and the office you're running for, but primarily your name.

Okay, so you have large posters for use on Election Day and for use as yard signs. Be respectful of other people's property, but be imaginative in looking for spaces where your poster will be appropriate. Then we have the smaller posters for use in doors. Next we come to a very important piece of material, your brochure.

The **brochure** is in many respects the key piece of literature you will use. There are many variations. You can have a brochure that you can use for general purposes, one on a card that you could use for Election Day which we sometimes call a handout. You may decide on one brochure that will do everything if your budget is limited, but my suggestion is to have at least two types of brochure. The first type is a two-sided, approximately 3" by 8" card with a panel on each side with your picture, name and office. This is almost a small version of your poster with your name the largest, most vivid item that you can use to pass out when you are talking to people quickly. You can also use that same item as an Election Day handout, and you should order large quantities based on expected voters, certainly for Election Day but also to give out in between. You can also have the second type, a larger brochure that would have several panels which might incorporate some of the material or all of the material from the card or handout. There are going to be people who will want to know more about you than the few words or pieces that we've described on the brief card. There are going to be people who will want to know something about you and your family. They will want to know what experiences you've had, or the community groups you belong to and they would also like perhaps to know your position on some issues. All of these things can be incorporated into a four or six panel brochure that can be used in large quantities to handout also.

I don't suggest giving out this particular brochure, the lengthier one, on Election Day because most people will not have a chance to read it. Maybe it could be available for the person who actually says "I want to know more," but that will be relatively rare. The main thing you will want to reach them with on Election Day is the handout panel as we've discussed it. Sometimes a small version with only the main information is used, 3x5" or less, and that is called a "palm card."

Discussion of the main brochure. We can spend some time on it because it's so important. In the first place it can be done by taking an 81/2" x 11" piece of paper and folding it into three panels, to give you an idea of how to visualize this brochure. It can be other sizes, other shapes, but this is a fairly basic format. The brochure should incorporate your color scheme, it should use any logo or symbol that you have. You could put a party symbol here, an elephant, a donkey, stars or stripes; you can invent your own symbol that you would like to be associated with. In general things that people *expect to see* are the best, and I don't think people expect political literature and materials to really be too innovative in their graphics. My suggestion is stick with the successful item, the things that people are used to seeing and associate positively with.

You may say, "Well, how do I design the brochure?" Designing any piece of literature is a cooperative process. My suggestion is this, if you have someone in your campaign to whom you've assigned this responsibility, still don't give up control of it completely. Remember it's your name, it's your image, your reputation, and ultimately your success or failure as a candidate that is at stake. Because you have a strong interest as a candidate or a manager in looking at a product, there are many stages in the printing process where you can stop the process long enough to look over what's being produced and make sure that it really is what you want.

This is what's called a proof and it is for the purpose of having you look over the printed material prior to its going into printing production. Today's printing technology allows you to look at options quickly and clearly. Once you okay it then it's your responsibility.

Many people feel that an election is not a real campaign unless there are **political buttons** for people to wear. People want buttons and if you don't have them they will perhaps feel that some ingredient is missing. So I would say, get your buttons, get them early, get them to have to give out to people who are for you. Don't be surprised if you never see too many people wearing them. Bumper stickers and buttons are two items in politics which almost every candidate feels that he must have, but of which far more are produced than are ever actually used. Nonetheless you probably should do them if you can afford it. With both buttons and bumper stickers the principle is the same, remember the name. You can put other information on there; elephants, donkeys, stars, stripes. Nonetheless that's just to give it flavor. The main thing that you have room for on these items is your name; first name in smaller letters, last name in larger letters and the office for which you are running. Usually a printer can arrange for buttons to be produced, or bumper stickers. If your printer is not familiar with how to get these things done, then your best bet is probably to obtain one of the catalogues of election material that, chances are, will be sent to you from a mailing list once you file to run. Most printers might have received such catalogs, and if you have an experienced campaign manager they will know where to look. With the internet, ordering materials is a few clicks away.

Most printing houses that produce political items can do so quickly if they are specialties and in many cases they have stock orders in which your name can simply be put onto a pre-existing format. That really saves a lot of design problems and you don't have to worry or argue about your design with your friends and volunteers and family and instead can concentrate on getting the message out.

What other kinds of materials are there? Some people like to use what they call strips. Strip signs are read from the top down at a vertical manner and are put on telephone poles or other similar locations. There are people who think this is a great idea, others feel it's ineffective. My own feeling is that which is read most normally, that is from left to right across is best, and that anything that varies from that is less desirable. Nonetheless it's an idea you might want to consider as an attention getter. Another thought for the brochure that you might want to consider is to have it be what is called a self-mailer, in other words you leave one panel of your brochure blank to use for an address and to send to people. If you work carefully with your printer and your media volunteers on the size, the content, you may find that this is a very efficient way to prepare a mailing piece.

It's an example how, if you plan your materials at the beginning, you can find many ways in which themes, design elements and other features can be carried throughout all of your materials. What about other **little handout items**? Bottle caps, matchbooks, pencils, pens, combs, nail files, rulers, you name it, if you can put your name on it, you can give it out as a political item, however you've got to think about the utility of this kind of item compared to other expenditures. Novelty items may be popular with kids, but how much they actually get your name out is something you will have to evaluate.

If you're going to attend firehouse dinners for example, or other political events where you could put out an item at each place, is it better to put out a comb, a matchbook, or what about one of your brochures? Perhaps sometimes it would be inappropriate or pushy to put out a brochure, but you would feel comfortable putting an item of minor value to someone; in that case it might be a good idea. Sometimes people get a trademark item, like a very successful candidate I know who used potholders in her first election. This was a very unique and useful item and it was a reminder of her unique qualities. The potholder became a trademark and even though over many years she ran for many other higher offices, many people still asked her for her potholders! Other candidates have other similar kinds of trademark items, although in general my advice would be to question carefully novelty items. If you see a use for them by all means go ahead, but make sure you don't spend too much time or money on things that are not going to give you the total return towards your goals.

Remember, the major criterion for judgment as you make all these decisions is what is the best use of limited money to get my name in people's minds so they'll vote for me on election day?

There are some other kinds of **promotional materials** you might want to think about. In these days of the popularity of t-shirts, try making them available or having them for your family, your friends, your supporters, and sometimes t-shirts can be used as a fundraising device. Have you ever heard of the term car top, in other words a sign which you put on the top of your car. There are different forms, some are fairly expensive. They do give you visibility. For example, when you look over the parking lot of the shopping center, and you can see the roofs of all the cars, if there's one big sign on top of a car that says, "Smith for City Council," it has a high degree of visibility and readability. Usually these car tops have suction cups and you can buy them commercially or you can make them yourself. In some areas you can rent the tops of taxi cabs, "taxi-tops," in which case you get the same effect as a sort of traveling billboard.

What about **billboards** themselves? In my experience commercial billboards look like something you might want to use, but usually by the time you get in a campaign, the time required to reserve a billboard is too lengthy or the cost is too much. Waiting time for the most popular locations may be considerable. If you happen to have an in with the company that controls the billboards, maybe that will be helpful, but chances are it's run by some out of town company which could care less about your timing schedule, therefore a lot of people don't get a chance to use billboards. Also they must be paid for in advance which is not always possible, and you'd be surprised how much they cost relative to other kinds of advertising. Companies may be willing to pay that when they have a product, but if you have to evaluate it versus other costs that may not be the way you choose to get your message out. If you do decide to use billboards make sure the layout is consistent with your overall theme. Don't waste it with cluttered pictures or lots of words. Make sure that it has primarily your name as the content (I know I sound like a broken record on this point!) and perhaps the office you're running for, perhaps a picture of you or your family. But most probably it should be you, and maybe a few theme words or your slogan. Don't try to put too much on a billboard. People glance at them quickly, usually as they're driving by, so don't try to distract them with lots of words or a complicated message.

If you're going to have **bumper stickers** keep a few things in mind. People generally are very protective of their cars. As we discussed when we talked about volunteers, many people who are for you will not necessarily feel that they want to go so far as to put a traveling message on their car. It's up to you or your workers to talk them into it, and I would suggest you don't try to pressure them. One way you can encourage people to display a bumper sticker is to have one that is made of vinyl. They cost a bit more, but on the other hand they come off much more easily. Most bumper stickers today are made of vinyl, and if you tell people this it makes them feel better about putting a bumper sticker on. Don't make a mistake that a friend of mine once made and have volunteers go throughout a parking lot at a political event, putting bumper stickers on everyone's car. It might seem like a clever thing to do, but even supportive people are offended when their car is plastered with a bumper sticker. The best thing to do is hand it to people. Also I'd say don't give a bumper sticker to someone unless they really tell you they're going to use it. If you have a list of volunteers you might want to send them out to the volunteers, since the idea is that they will be more likely to use them than the average person. But even at a political event of your own supporters, I think you'll find that many people honestly tell you they'd rather not put one on. In that case, it's better not to waste them.

Still you have to give out many to see a few on, and as I've said before don't be discouraged as you drive around the streets of your town and you try to figure out where all those bumper stickers went. A few last thoughts about bumper stickers; one is, remember that you can display a bumper sticker on the window of your car and perhaps achieve more visibility than if it's on your bumper. And also if you think about it, far more people see the front bumper of your car than see the rear bumper...but since you're more likely to have time to look when you're stopped, or are in parking lots, rear mounting is the more traditional placement.

A final word on advertising. In everything you do, in all media, make sure your name and your accompanying themes are represented. If your slogan that you've adopted is, "John Smith for lower taxes," or "Jane Smith for a more active city council," put that on each item that you print or produce, so that it begins to reinforce the idea that you have already planted in people's minds. The more you can do that, the more **reinforcement** you achieve throughout the whole set of materials, all the way through. From the first brochure a person gets when they hear about you, or the first ad or sign they see, all the way to election day when they show up at the polls, when they see the same name, the same face, and most importantly the same theme, that will take your message cumulatively to success.

B. Public Relations

Next let's talk about the other type of communications, **Public relations or "PR."** These are the communications that you and your campaign do not control directly, although you and your team will do your best to get your message out through others in the way you want it to be. You want to get "covered" by the media as much as possible on your terms, still remembering name and theme is a major goal.

First let's talk about seeking **endorsements** from newspapers. Radio and television stations generally do not endorse candidates. Because they have a monopoly on the particular frequencies they're licensed to use, they generally make far more effort to provide balanced coverage, and to provide access to advertising from all candidates. Such is not the case for newspapers. Newspapers often endorse, although sometimes they don't. Sometimes in a hot, local race, the newspaper really is unable to choose between the candidates, or makes a specific policy decision not to choose one over the other even though personally the editor or owner might favor a particular candidate. Even if you are not endorsed and another candidate is, you may want to advertise in the paper to reach the readers directly and thus "go around" the choice of the paper. A good ad is probably read by more readers than editorial endorsements. It is my feeling that newspapers are over-rated as influencers of voters, and the fact that you, your opponent, and all of your workers may avidly read everything about the election doesn't necessarily mean it is reaching more than a fraction of the electorate. Obviously in a small town with only one newspaper, an election race could be greatly affected by it; in large metropolitan areas, your race may be a "footnote" to the big metro dailies and your community weekly newspaper may be your best bet for coverage. You have to judge the media situation in your own district or town and act accordingly.

The "news" aspect of the media. Whether or not the newspaper endorses, it is still a good idea to seek out a meeting with the editors as well as the reporters of that particular newspaper. You or your communications worker should make it a point, during the earlier stages of the campaign, such as in the months of September or early

October before the customary November election, to call and set up an appointment about the time when newspapers begin covering the campaign, or may begin to write about the campaign editorially. In many cases, you will sit down with an editor or an editorial board of more than one person, and usually it would include the reporter who covers politics and specifically your race.

Sitting down and ranging over the issues with them, talking about the strategy that you're following in your campaign, you will often get some very good questions from these people. It is your opportunity to shine. The better you do, the more likely are to either get an endorsement or if not an endorsement, at least a favorable reference in the editorial pages. I'm not saying that a good interview would necessarily get you better or more "favorable" news coverage. But I have found that if the editors and reporters feel you are doing a fair job and an energetic job of portraying your views, and that you can do so articulately, it certainly will result in more coverage and perhaps, if not sympathetic, at least positive coverage in that newspaper.

Press releases. Press releases are statements that you or your staff write up. They should be on your letterhead, neatly produced, and ordinarily very simple. They should make your statement in the context of a favorable description, and any facts you care to include. A press release could state an announcement you are making, a view you're expressing or an appearance that you will make or have already made. You can call, fax, or email to newspapers, radio and television stations on the telephone or by email, to make your statement or directly state a press release. You can follow up with mailed or delivered copies if you want to "make a record" of your input but that is often not necessary.

Of course, one of your lists that you need is an accurate up-to-date press list. When you put out a press release, make sure that you put a telephone number and the name of a person to be contacted, including yourself if further comments are desired. It's nice to have someone in your organization who specializes in the press. You may have discovered the perfect person who can call reporters on the phone and talk to them,arrange to have interviews with you, write press releases. But I have found in my campaigns that I often have to be my own spokesman. You are your own best spokesman. If the media in your area are not too numerous, it doesn't hurt to have phone conversations with the reporters or editors who are covering the story or to provide your opinions for stories they're writing. But press releases are often helpful even if you're talking to reporters. They may jot down what you're saying, but it's nice to have it in writing too. The press release offers you the opportunity to put down exactly what you want to say.

The normal press release in a local campaign should be one page long, possibly two and for some really complicated topics, maybe three maximum. The press release should answer all the questions that a reporter asks himself as he writes the story, namely, as they say in journalism school, the "five w's:" **who, what, when, why and where.** Most newspaper people will not write a story that incorporates your press release directly. But the more work a reporter is expected to do, the more they will find a news release a real aid in preparing their story. And you may find that in many smaller papers such as weeklies where one or two people put the whole thing together, if you have a well prepared press release, it may go in verbatim.

If a **photo** goes along with the story, then you should provide an opportunity for the paper to take a photo or provide one yourself. One piece of advice is to get a good shot of yourself, and the best way to do that is to find what you want or get several options from which to choose the one that's best. Critique it, have your family and friends critique it. Try and ask yourself if this shot conveys the image that you are looking to put forward to the public. Spend the money if necessary, to have a good "stock shot" of yourself taken. And have plenty of copies on hand. If you are running a kind of folksy campaign in which a smile is appropriate, that is fine. On the other hand, if you are running a serious campaign or you are younger and want to look more experienced, you may want to go with a more serious pose.

Press conferences. Sometimes the importance of your views or the content of an announcement that you are making, will make a press conference advisable in addition to a press release. In this case, you call the members of the press and let them know, as much in advance as possible, where and when the press conference will take place. If you can, have coffee or light refreshments for them. Certainly try to create a friendly and businesslike environment in which you can state your viewpoint.

Always answer questions in a forthright and amiable manner. Be confident. Don't be upset by seemingly hostile questions from a member of the press. In my experience, you're going to be judged almost as much by reporters for your attitude and manner in answering questions, as what you actually say.

If you do not want to be quoted, you must make that a precondition for going further in the interview. Always be clear if you want to go off the record. You must have a clear under-standing with the reporter and you should not ever attack individuals and you should be able to explain background without going on the record, if that is the understanding of both you and the reporter. Generally speaking however, my best advice is, that it's better not to go off the record. Two other pieces of advice when dealing with reporters, if you do not know the answer to a question, honestly say so and get back to the reporter when you can get the information. And never, ever lie to a reporter. Both advertising and public relations are aimed at communicating your message. Your message is the total impression you want to make. It must be reinforced through every possible means and it should be clear. It should establish the theme and reiterate the theme and end up with people understanding through all the ways you have communicated with them, what your campaign is all about. You have to take your cues on how to reach the press and communicate with them, from those who cover the campaign. Whether it's the fax, email, telephone, in person, let them give you the ideas about how they like to be reached and which of these forms of communication you can use.

C.   Electronic Media

Speaking of email, we need to keep in mind one category of communication that has grown in usage and impact on the political process, the use of the internet in addition to email, websites, the use of blogs and social networking.

These techniques haven't replaced the other forms of communication, but they have added a new dimension to campaigning--as to every other function of society, whether keeping in touch with other people, shopping, becoming informed or being entertained.

Like many other ways of reaching people, which is what all of our means of outreach are intended to do, we can place too much or too little emphasis on this electronic category. Don't expect it to be some magical technique which is going to revolutionize your race, but also don't underestimate the amount of exposure and reinforcement that you can gain from it, particularly among those of the younger age brackets with whom it's very popular. It has the additional advantage of being economical. You're not paying in the case of electronic media for the medium, only for getting your message on to it.

Let's start with your **website**. Find a web designer if you don't know one. These days so many people have business or personal websites, you can ask around about what person or firm seems to do a good job in your area. They could be local. They could be remote. (Although I always feel it's good to be able to interact with someone face to face, both to select them and to consult with them as needed.) Your website should obviously have all the usual navigation tools and tabs. If you're not sure what it should look like, visit some sites that are currently in use as campaign or candidate sites and then review the ideas or techniques you like the best with your designer.

If you're a party or organization-sponsored candidate, you might want to be featured on that organization or party's website. But don't rule out the advantage that you might gain by being independent of that party or organization by having your own individual presence on the internet.

You should probably accept the idea that most people will go to your website because you, your workers or your advertising, "drive" people to the website as they say. Your internet address should be in all the literature. On the website, you can inform people, persuade people, have them sign up as volunteers, inform the press and that most important aspect, raise money for your campaign. View your website as a virtual headquarters, open 24/7 which functions without even having to be manned.

Somebody has to update the website and check the website every day. This is very important. One of your volunteers or more if necessary, should perform this duty and have the ability to add new material, for example, about your public schedule or favorable news articles, or press releases for the press. You can upload photos of you on the campaign trail and feature people who will give a testimony for you either in print, on the website or on an audio or video clip. You can have photos there for the press to pick up as well.

Those same volunteers or different ones if you have enough volunteers, should be assigned to follow your internet presence, whether it's your material, material from a neutral source, a news organization or even from your opponent or detractors. Always take the attitude that your opponent and his or her organization are monitoring not only their own candidate but also you and any other opponents of theirs.

With the anonymity of the internet there are people who will take it upon themselves (with or without the actual blessing of the candidate, whether you or others) to post information or opinions and sometimes what they refer to as facts, on the internet.

Some of this internet chatter simply adds interest and life to the campaign. But it can be a form of attack. It's distracting and hard to get a grip on how to best respond. It's my opinion that most people will go to a website to gain either preliminary or sometimes more detailed information on the topic of their search. But they don't want to get bogged down in a long string of cross-references and minute items of back and forth arguments. On the other hand, there is a small element of people which does have that desire and are attracted to it. It's a newer, faster and more edgy form of letters to the editor in the local newspaper.

Letters to the editor, in my opinion, and the internet chat crowd, are basically a small self-selected group of people who are intensely involved and get their kicks out of this type of argument. Don't ignore it but also don't let it get to you and throw you off your positive track and all your other techniques of campaigning and communicating that are reaching far more people.

Email is a new form of communicating to large groups. But many people don't welcome strangers dropping into their email on spams or other kinds of group email which are already invaded by marketers of all kinds. If you have lists from friendly groups that you feel would be accepting, then use it. But I'd be leery of trying to replace normal, direct mail, whether letters or other campaign literature pieces, with email. If someone comes to your website, they've come there on their own and are curious to some degree. If you want to invite visitors to your site to communicate directly with you by direct response on the website, telephone, email, you can give them that information.

67

<u>You can always use all your other forms of communication to remind or inform readers of your web presence, so it becomes a true networking tool.</u> Should you have a blog? Sure. But remember what sounds easy and not very time-consuming, can become a burden in effort and time if you are pulled many different ways and have a busy schedule. Most large campaigns these days have an electronic media volunteer, staff person or consultant whose job it is to enter and possibly compose your latest information and blog update. Facebook, Twitter and all the other systems of social networking, are often used today to attract or retain a following for those for whom **social network** sites are important. If you're on them, you can quickly sense how you could use them for event promotion, fundraising, news flashes, endorsements by others and driving traffic to your website. If you're not part of the social networking scene, find people, family members, friends or volunteers who will acquaint you with it and who might enjoy helping you expand your presence on the social networks.

Chapter Five

Presenting Yourself

Image + Speaking + Debates + Names + Family Members + Reaching People + Create A Network + Feeling At Home Wherever You Are

Our next chapter is presenting yourself; how to present you and your image to the voters. We cover image, speaking, debates, how to handle them, names, family members and then we move onto how to reach people, how to create a network and finally in this section, how to feel at home wherever you are. Presenting yourself is an important part of running to win. How you portray your qualities and your sense of self have an important impact on your campaign because they tell other people a lot about you and how you feel about yourself.

A. Image

First let's consider **your image**. Everybody has their own personality and everybody has their own look. We're probably not going to change the basic patterns of a lifetime in the interest of one election. Nonetheless, there are a few points that maybe you haven't needed to think about in your daily life up until now, that do bear on the way people think about you. If you're not sure you believe image is a critical component of your campaign, think of the recent experiment reported by David Brooks in which pairs of photos of actual gubernatorial opposing candidates were shown to those who had no knowledge of the races. The winners were chosen 70% of the time!

In the first place, remember, people expect those in public office to be conventional and perhaps a bit more formal. They expect people in public office to be like other people in the business world. If you have habits or dress preferences that are outside the normal mode, you're going to attract some attention. I'm not saying you're going to lose. I'm not saying you're going to be unpopular. But the fact is, for both men and women, people expect those who are running for office to dress with a little more formality than the average person. The so-called dress for success outfit of the dark suit with white or pastel shirt and appropriate accessories is always acceptable. For men, striped or patterned, relatively conservative, tie, with black shoes and socks, is pretty standard advice. Women have more flair expected. This doesn't mean that everybody should follow this kind of advice. In your area, people may wear different kinds of dress, perhaps less formal than I've described. But in general, it's fair to say that even though someone else may dress a certain way as an individual, they may expect those in public office to dress a little more formally, a little more business-like. Remember, this is a democracy. If you want to be involved in governing in a democracy, then don't resent it if other people want you to live up to their expectations. Part of representing people is for them to be comfortable with you.

Yes, it does mean that you may have to dampen your own individuality a bit. If it bothers you to do this, perhaps you shouldn't be running. But I think you can make a compromise in which you retain your own personality, your own beliefs and your lifestyle, but on the other hand you do it in a way that isn't inconsistent with being seen as conventionally acceptable. You can be like other people in many ways but also meeting their expectations for the way someone who aspires to office should appear.

How about the way you handle yourself? You have to think of yourself as being a little bit more forward when running for office. After all, people are going to expect you to articulate on their behalf. They want to know what you have to say about the issues that may be on their mind. **They want to feel that you can express their feelings**. Think of this when you go into a group and have an opportunity to speak with people, either to the group as a whole or to individuals. What is it that you can say that will express their thoughts in a way that will allow them to say to themselves, "John Smith can speak for me." Sometimes it may be the thoughts you have about issues that are unrelated to the campaign issues that are of interest to them. They might want to know how you feel about bringing up your children, or what's good for your neighborhood, and that will help them have an impression of you as someone who will talk to them about the issues that are important in life, can express the thoughts that think are important. They don't always have to agree with your thoughts to respect them, although obviously the more agreement you can find with a person, the more they are likely to think that you're quite intelligent.

71

We've talked about presenting yourself through written materials. Now let's talk about presenting yourself in person.

B. Speaking

Speaking. In the course of your life, in school, in clubs, and your business, you may have spoken to groups, large or small, quite a bit. If that's the case, you're very lucky because that means you won't have that sense of fear that candidates sometimes have about putting their message into words and presenting it to others, especially in groups. People often remember that sense of tension when in school they were required to stand up in front of the class; others take to it like a duck to water. No matter what category you're in, speaking can become a natural and positive part of your campaign and style.

Even for those of us who are experienced, still we need to think carefully as we prepare to go out and talk in public. There are many dangers. For example, don't appear to boast or brag or talk too much about how great you are. On the other hand, one of the things that you must do even though it's sometimes uncomfortable, is to say positive, favorable things about yourself. In fact, it's only through practice that you're going to be most comfortable about what you say about yourself and your candidacy.

One of the best ways to improve your speaking ability is to have a friend videotape or film you giving your standard "talk" and then sitting down to watch yourself with a small group of your choosing, perhaps spouse and close campaign

72

leaders. You will be your own best critic, and the others can discuss with you what needs improving and how to do it.

As I approach any audience, whether it's a group of hundreds at a dinner or a meeting of only ten or 20 people in someone's living room, there are certain elements that I try to cover.

One is, **who am I?** A few comments that associate you with that group to whom you are talking are important in answering this question. What is your connection with them? How do you know the people who are gathered in front of you? Then you want to cover the question, **why am I running?** This will lead naturally into the next section, which is, **what do I want to do in office?** What are the challenges that lay before the person who will hold this office and the town or jurisdiction in which you're running. What are the issues confronting this jurisdiction? School district? Your state? And how will you try to deal with those issues?

Don't try to talk about too much. It's better to restrict your talk to a few of the main issues and the main challenges. Some people feel that they have to show off their knowledge of every last policy involved with the office. My suggestion is, try not to do that. Remember, after you're finished speaking, those who want more details can always come up to you on their own. In fact, when I'm speaking, I usually say somewhere in my speech, "For those of you who want to talk in more detail, I will stick around after I'm through the formal speaking." Obviously, if you have to move on, you can't do that but if you possibly can, try to arrange it. People will be impressed, and many people who fear asking you a question in public will be happy to ask you a question in private, or to say a supportive word or to give you a suggestion and of course, to offer to volunteer.

73

Here are a few tips about speaking. Don't speak too fast. People sometimes have a tendency to want to say everything in a short time. Speak more slowly than you would normally speak so that people have a chance to hear and absorb what you're saying. In my experience, very rarely should an informal speech last more than five or ten minutes and very rarely should a formal speech exceed 15 or 20 minutes. Another opinion I have is that questions and answers engage the audience much more than just your speaking. That's why if you can make a few comments and then have questions and answers it will do several things. It will give people a chance to let you know what's on their minds. It will give them a sense of participation. It will also give them the feeling that you have the confidence to open yourself up and take questions that you may not have known about an advance. Naturally, you should try to anticipate what questions a group might have. But remember, you don't have to know everything. You don't have to claim to know everything. If asked a question that you are not ready to handle, it's better to be honest and say, "I don't know the answer to that question but I'll find out and let you know." And then get the person's name or card and get back to them. This will certainly make a favorable impression on them.

Remember, most people do not know too much about the office you're running for or its responsibilities. Maybe if there's a big issue involved they focus on that. But in many cases, there are many other parts of the job that are basically uninteresting to most people. In other words, you will be the one telling most people not only that you want to run for a certain job but why that job is important and why it matters to them who gets the job and what that job entails. That's a lot that you have to accomplish in a short period of time in which to speak. Try your talk out on your family or your friends. Try your ideas out on them. Construct a short talk which you can use in almost any circumstances and you'll improve that as you go along. You'll find there are some things that you say that people really like. They may applaud a little more loudly or laugh a little bit more when they hear what you're saying and that will tell you what parts to keep in your talk. Maybe you'll find that some parts tend to bore an audience and you'll know that you can drop those or make them a little more brief.

Don't be thrown off by what a friend of mine calls "banana peels", such as a mike not working or a baby crying or even a hostile question or a heckler. Be calm. Be open. Make a humorous remark and move on. Turn off a noisy or dead mike and speak without it. People will be impressed that you could handle an uncomfortable situation. One of the things you do need is a friend or staff member, one who will tell you honestly whether you're doing a good job in your speech, just as with any of your other responsibilities as a candidate. You need someone who will not be too polite to tell you the things that might be unpleasant or that they think that you might not want to hear. Be alert to criticism because that's how you improve.

Much that is in your standard talk can also be used in interviews with the press or groups with whom you meet, sometimes with rephrasing, emphasis or elaboration. Be as conversational as you can be and relaxed (or at least appear to be relaxed) in your interviews or appearances. Try to be comfortable in your public role.

C.   Debates

Should you **debate** your opponent? In today's political world, that question is being asked more and more often. Whether it's the candidates for president debating on national television or a school board or legislative candidate debating in front of the local Chamber of Commerce. So let's think first about this question: what is a debate?.

In the first place, sometimes an invitation to a joint appearance may not be billed as a debate but it could become one so you will have to think in terms of debate any time you are invited to appear with your opponent; sometimes by a neutral group such as a Chamber of Commerce or by a newspaper. For the most part, such groups may ask candidates to appear by themselves one at a time, hoping to hear from both candidates. But sometimes groups will invite both or all candidates at the same time.

Debates are usually labeled as debates that are intended to be a confrontation between two or more opponents, in which they will either be asked questions by a panel, by a single moderator or sometimes by the audience. Sometimes there might even be a call-in debate on a local radio or television station so there is a variety of forms in which debates can take place.

You will have to decide early in your campaign whether you are going to accept an invitation if you get it or whether to issue a challenge. It doesn't hurt to think ahead of time about what your response is going to be if you anticipate receiving such an invitation. Sometimes a candidate challenges the other to a debate. If that might be the case, at the very inception of your candidacy, one of the things that you should talk to your core group of advisors may be this question; should you challenge your opponent? Or if your opponent challenges you, should you accept?

If you are going to extend a challenge or accept a challenge, what are the circumstances under which you would like the debate to take place? My feeling has always been when I'm a candidate that basically I'll go anywhere that a group wants to hear me on the theory that I will present my case in the best favorable way. I may or I may not gain any new voters but then even in a group that might be expected to be unfriendly, I may win over a few people to my point of view or at least impress them that I had the courage or the courtesy to come. I feel the same way about a debate. If you have enough confidence in your views and your ability to express them in argument, then there's no reason to refuse to attend any setting where with or without opponents, you have the chance to speak.

But always weigh the benefits of a particular appearance carefully. Sometimes what is billed as a debate may get very boring because usually what each candidate tries to do is to give his own set responses as you should. In any campaign, it is pretty predictable what the questions are going to be and what the differences are between the candidates. Very few surprises develop in a campaign that has been going on for any length of time in terms of what you or the other candidates are likely to say. Make sure you get in the points that allow you to develop your theme. Chances are that the press and the public have asked the same questions so that each candidate ought to know what he is going to say. But it is possible in a debate setting that there may be detailed questions or new questions that might challenge either or both of the participants in some way they haven't been before. They may have to wing it. That's when debates can turn into disasters for candidates who have not anticipated what the questions might be.

So, if you are going into a debate setting, make sure you have anticipated the questions and practiced the answers. You might even want to go to the extent of having a dry run with your advisors. But remember, it is possible for you to over prepare. Don't get so involved in trying to memorize detailed facts that you clutch and cannot be relaxed. Remember, President Reagan, who did so effectively in the campaign debate of 1980, later in 1984 in his first debate was widely thought to have experienced exactly what I described. He over prepared and the advisors he had were so interested in prepping him on details, they forgot that President Reagan's great strength as a communicator was that he was someone who could state simply and in good humor, broad truths in a way the American people could understand. Keep that in mind. And of course, in the second debate of 1984, he again appeared in exactly his traditional manner, won the debate and clinched the campaign.

Debates are not usually the sole decisive factor in an election. Where publicity comes to rest on a debate, what could happen in a local race where the press focuses attention on it and the tension runs high, it could take on a fair amount of significance in the press reports. So you do need to think about whether you want to debate, what kind of debate you would like to have. And sometimes you can accept an invitation from a third party, even from the opponent if you want to, but you still retain the control to specify how it will take place and what the rules will be. Always retain as much control as possible. Many times, at a debate in these days of media emphasis, the main people who are attracted either to attend the debate or who follow it, are those who are most attuned to the race and often those who are most committed to you or to your opponent.

I even heard one very effective local candidate say at a debate, he wanted to thank his supporters and his opponent's supporters because without them there wouldn't be too many people there. That's all too true but nonetheless, do not minimize the effects that could come from making a mistake or doing a poor job. There are many people, experts in politics who feel that a debate can hurt you in a negative way if you make a mistake far more than it could help you in a positive manner. The press reports give the debate far more attention than for those present. One final pointer, if you are naturally polite in your conversational manner, be prepared to find in a joint interview or debate that your opponent may try to talk over you or your answers. I'd say let them get away with this once. But if the moderator doesn't step in to enforce fairness, then you can chide the opponent firmly and openly such as by saying, "I let you talk, now you let me." Or else talk right along with your opponent if he tries to use your time or intimidate you.

D. Names

Names. You're in the business of names. You want people to remember your name and much of your campaign revolves around accomplishing that. So it is logical to say to help remember your name, it would be helpful to you if you can remember those of others.

Not everybody in politics has a good memory for names, but my guess is that those who are most successful have either the luck, or have trained themselves, to be able to remember other peoples' names. When you go out in the street, when you go to a meeting, when you have a party, all of these are times that people may be saying to themselves, "Does John Smith remember me?" For those who are your personal friends, this is no problem. But, of course, you want to make many, many new friends, in the course of a campaign, who will picture themselves as having a close relationship with you.

My suggestion is try to remember names, but don't be so intense about it that you clutch, or become nervous about it. It's better to admit that you don't remember somebody's name, embarrassing though it sometimes may be, than to call somebody by the wrong name. I must say, I have occasionally done this, and it's a feeling you'd rather not have. One way to avoid that is if you are setting up an event, or someone is setting it up for you, **use nametags**. It's one of the easiest ways, not only to help you identify people, and remind you of their names, but it also has the function of helping other people at an event relate to the people who are there. It's amazing how many times people will say, "I saw so and so, and I'm supposed to know them, but I couldn't remember their name, so I didn't talk to them." Of course, that's the exact opposite of what a social event should be!

An event should be a chance for people to get to know each other, or if they know each other already, to know each other better, and certainly to know you. So to me, nametags are well worth the effort to have people put them on when they come in. You can have a volunteer, perhaps, help them put their nametags on when they enter, but there's nothing wrong with leaving nametags and a pen out if the event is small enough. If you are arranging the event, you can stand a little further inside the room, so that by the time people get to you, they will have their nametags on. That way you can quickly check them if there's any doubt. Of course, if the event is not one where you have that control, you just have to do the best you can. I found that people understand, for the most part, when politicians might make a mistake, or don't always remember them. The best thing is to just be open about it. Apologize if it's a mistake, and try to get the name in your mind so that you won't do it again.

Never hesitate to introduce yourself to others who may not know you. If you say, "I'm John Smith," it invites the other person to give their name. If they do know you, they can say, "Oh, of course, I know you." Or you can do the same thing with them. Many times you will remember them, but maybe if you didn't quite remember the name, it's considerate to make sure that you introduce yourself. You sometimes get that person who says, "You don't know who I am, do you?" You will have a choice when this happens. Often with people like this, I say, "No. I don't. Who are you?" Sometimes people like that are so insensitive that this honesty doesn't bother them. Even if I do remember them, I almost feel like saying, "I don't" anyway. When you run into people like this, you just have to deal with them the best you can. Not every, single person that you meet or have contact with is making a critical difference in your campaign. I guess you should approach the issue this way. <u>You do need each and every last vote, because all of the individual votes add up. But nonetheless, if you find that you do unintentionally slight someone, if you've done the best you can, and you're trying to be nice, just let it go at that.</u>

E. Family Members

Family members. Sometimes the election of a member of their family is exciting to those related to a candidate. Other times, they're either too young to know what is going on, or perhaps disinterested, and don't feel they have a stake in an election. Many candidates in the past have felt that their wives contributed significantly to their ability to be elected, or husbands, as the case may be. The support, friendship and advice that comes from your loved ones will be very valuable to you. Certainly, their ability to campaign with you can extend your own personality, as it were, beyond what you could do yourself.

My wife has shared some thoughts with me for this chapter and as you will see I am drawing on them extensively.

I have often found that if there are two or three events in one night, which sometimes happens during a busy campaign period, that I would choose to go to a newer group, or a group involving an issue oriented presentation where I, as a candidate, should be. Whereas with a more social occasion, or a group with whom I am very familiar, my wife can go and represent me with no feeling on anyone's part that they have been slighted. A candidate, himself, is usually the desired person to attend events, but I have found that most groups understand, especially during a busy period, that one person cannot be in every place at one time.

Often a devoted family member can represent you far better than sending someone with no identifiable status. Of course, these decisions must be made carefully and with a lot of information and understanding of how the groups involved will react. I know my wife tells me it is sometimes difficult when she attends a meeting with me, and I am speaking, to always look like she is paying rapt attention, and like she agrees with everything I am saying! I think it is important for a spouse to be friendly and supportive in public settings, as well as in private, but it's very important that the frank and candid advice your spouse will give you should be done in private and not in public. You can overdo the loving spouse routine, but in our family oriented society, people, whether it's fair or unfair, do want to know about your family, as well as yourself. They want to know how many children you have, where they go to school.

In fact, they may even be interested in such things as whether my wife works, or not, or what her beliefs are about certain things. As I covered previously, the answer to these questions may mean as much to potential voters as your stands on the specific issues that are involved in the election. Obviously, your children and your spouse should have a good appearance in terms of their dress and their mannerisms. Certainly many times they will be expected to meet people in the same friendly vein as you are. When this happens, they should be fully prepared. They should put on the hat of the candidate, as it were, just as you are, and try to be as gracious and friendly as possible. It will be of inestimable value to your campaign. Everything I've said about your immediate family, of course, can also be extended to your parents and other members of your extended family, if they care to be involved.

Often people ask my wife what I think about something, as if she knows my position on every issue. She has worked out a method of answering questions like this. Sometimes she says that she doesn't know. Other times she says she thinks that I feel a certain way. Or if it is something on which there is a very clear identification of my position, especially if it's been published or made public, she can state it in exactly that way. But she also makes it clear to people that she is not speaking for me, and if she has any reservation at all, she refers them to me, and in a friendly manner conveys the idea that although she is interested in the race, and wants to be helpful, that she is not trying to run, herself, or assume the responsibility of the office. This is a ticklish position for someone to be in. In fact, it's probably much harder for my wife to be the candidate's wife than it is for me to be the candidate when it comes to certain kinds of questions. Often my wife receives phone calls during a campaign in which people ask her, when she says that I'm out campaigning, what her response is, or her advice on a particular question. It could be a campaigner or supporter. In some cases it could be from an inquiring voter who is trying to make up their mind. She tries to give the appropriate answer and has learned to size up the caller and determine which calls to go further on, and which to simply take a message. She also told me that often she has had friendly talks with reporters, or others, who call trying to find me. She doesn't go out of her way to do this, but where they have initiated conversations, and she either knows them or senses sincere interest, she has often been able to help create a favorable atmosphere for my eventual talk with such a person by being friendly.

Without being able to give specific advice, a little experience will probably go a long way in helping people decide whether they want to play a somewhat active role in a campaign. There are many successful political candidates who do not choose to involve their wives, husbands, or children in their campaigns. And there are some spouses who choose, on their own, not to become part of a process that may not interest them. In many cases if the candidate's wife, for example, is quite happy with her own life and does not choose to participate, or a husband who may be helpful to a candidate, but does not desire to get involved in the campaign, these may be quite satisfactory relationships, as long as they are understood by all involved. If a man candidate is appearing at a woman's group, it's often extremely helpful to be able to take his wife with him, and I'm sure the same thing would apply to a woman candidate going to a men's group.

In addition to attending public appearances with the candidate, other areas in which a spouse may be valuable would be support in private and in the campaign work, itself. As far as supporting the candidate, I know my wife has often been a sounding board for ideas, and listened to me vent my frustrations, and helped create a calm environment in which I could frankly discuss something that was on my mind. That kind of assistance is hard to overestimate. I know that during campaign periods, my wife has often helped organize the family, not for me to avoid my responsibilities, but to make sure that to the extent possible, things that would create a conflict with the campaign were minimized as much as could be. Any spouse can be, in that respect, the most valuable person of those around the candidate.

As far as campaign support, I have found a candidate's wife is somewhat like a minister's wife, as the old saying goes: "If she sings in the choir, she wants to take over everything. If she doesn't sing in the choir, then she doesn't participate." A candidate's spouse should show that she or he is able and willing to do anything that anyone else is expected to do in the campaign.

Depending on your own situation and organization, some-times a spouse may inhibit frankness in small group strat-egy meetings of your organization, if others hold back from disagreeing with him or her. But on the other hand everyone recognizes the personal stake they have in the outcome and understands the key advisory status they have. This is something for you to work out together as you decide how to best function as a couple in the campaign.

Often in a smaller, low cost campaign, it is the candidate and his family who end up doing a lot of the work. I've already discussed this under the candidate's responsibility, and the same thing applies to the wife, husband or children. You are asking other people to volunteer to do tasks, and it really makes them feel good and appreciative if they are joined in whatever they are doing by the candidate's family members. Those so close to the candidate can not only participate with the other volunteers, but the family members can also thank the volunteers in a special way, while working together.

One thing about children is that candidates sometimes think that people want to see their children attend events. This may be true, but chances are they don't always. I would say that any event of a formal nature is probably inappropriate for children under fifteen. You have to gauge the maturity level of your own children, but that's been my experience. I haven't wanted to alienate my kids from politics, because I want them to understand it and appreciate it, but I also don't want them to feel imposed upon by it. They do their share of work during a campaign, but I also try not to overdo the expectations that I have on them for going to events. I have found that events that are informal, or if there are games, or time for social interaction with other children, or if there's food, usually those things indicate it's more of an event for children to enjoy. People do want to see your children, and they do want, as we might imagine, to judge them for their looks and their behavior, but it also gives them a chance to assess you and the job that you and your spouse have done in rearing your children. Whether this is fair or unfair, it is a measure in our society that people like to be familiar with those who are close to you.

Your instructions to your children ought to be to behave well, naturally. I almost feel that the more you try to instruct kids on what to say or do, the more counterproductive it sometimes is. One suggestion my wife has made, that she has followed over the years, is if you are both going to an event, where you both need to participate, and the children are expected to be there, or you have decided you want them there, it is really helpful if you can take a friend, perhaps a grown teenager or family member, who can watch the children while you and your spouse are working on your obligations yourselves.

Keep in mind one thing when the two of you go together to an event, if it is a reception, a cocktail party, or some type of event where you're both expected to mingle with the crowd, if you stay together that may be easier for many couples. But my wife and I have developed a practice of heading off in different directions. When the event is over, we get back together either at the event or in the car going home and, of course, have a chance to discuss what we've learned, or the people we've met. One advantage is you're going to gain twice as much information. You're going to make twice as many contacts if you both are doing the meeting of other people, rather than just staying together. Sometimes my wife has a chance to talk to other people that I didn't get a chance to see, and sometimes people will tell her things that they wouldn't tell me, ironic as that might seem. So I guess it all boils down to that cliché, as with any marriage, a candidacy in which you both are involved, is a teamwork effort, and that is very satisfying.

Another area in which my wife has been very helpful is when I am recruiting volunteers for the campaign, and there are many calls to be made. You may have a volunteer chairman, who is doing a lot of recruiting, or following up on contacts that you make, but I have found it is a big help as a substitute for having the candidate call, which is probably the best thing in recruiting, to have the candidate's spouse call. From what my wife has said to me, it is far easier for someone to say "No" to just another campaign worker than it is to say "No" to the candidate, or the candidate's spouse.

F.   Reaching People

Reaching People. Always try, even if you can't speak at an event, to be publicly introduced. Sometimes this is a little bit of a problem, and you'll want to be alert on how to handle this most sensitively. It doesn't come naturally to be pushy. On the other hand, remember, for your candidacy to be successful, you do need to be clear with people, when they are sponsoring events, that you would like to be introduced, and that it would be helpful for you to be introduced. It's your name that you want people to remember and to associate it with you. If you can simply stand up and give a friendly wave, especially at a non-political gathering where a talk might be inappropriate, or perhaps even a reference to your political aspirations, that will still help get the word out.

Remember, the problem is not telling people who are involved in politics about your race. They will know about it already. It's the group of people who are likely to vote, who have friends who are likely to vote, that you want to reach. Many are not deeply involved themselves but who are alert and will learn, if you tell them, and it is to them that you reach out. That means that sometimes you will have to let people know clearly in your church or synagogue, in your social club, service club or any group that you belong to, in a nice, polite, not in a pushy way, but you would value their support for this office.

Remember politics is based on the idea that if people know you, know about you and what you stand for, or even if they don't know what you stand for, but they like you and trust you, they will be more likely to vote for you than not.

Sometimes people who know us don't like us, or don't like our views. Maybe in that case exposure to them, or a reminder to them, is not going to be helpful. However, the law of averages is on your side. Most people appreciate learning that you're running. They appreciate the fact that you care about their vote and their opinion. That will carry over into their thinking as they go to the polls, as they enter the voting booth to make that critical decision. As part of reaching people, let's talk about your interaction with other people.

You're talking to them. You're meeting them. Many of us take for granted these everyday transactions we have with other people, but let's just think for a moment about even such basic things as the handshake or chatting with people. When you meet someone, there are things to keep in mind to help your candidacy. Study your own habits so that you can improve them if necessary. One of the things about running for public office is that people expect you to take the lead with them. In other words, don't be afraid to introduce yourself. If you go into a room, and there are many people there, look on that as an opportunity to win over all those people. Besides introducing yourself, you may have to initiate conversations with those who may be shy. Part of what you're doing is simply meeting each person. Try to make that your aim. When you go into a room, try to meet, talk with, and introduce yourself to every person in that room. It means you can't linger in long conversations with specific individuals, especially people you know, and who, let's face it, are for you already and are going to vote for you.

Let's tackle it with this goal in mind. Walk up to someone. Extend your hand. Give them a firm handshake, and people will judge you by that. Take it a little easier on those who are less able to take a hearty handshake, like children or elderly people. Nonetheless, let them know you're there. You can say over and over if necessary, but hopefully fresh each time, "I'm Jane Smith. I'm running for county commissioner." And then add, "I hope you'll vote for me on election day, May third." This may help make that a specific time in their mind that they might not be aware of, or use any other line that you're comfortable with, or that works into your campaign, such as, "I hope you'll support me," or, "We need a change." Sometimes the person will say, "I'm pleased to meet you." Sometimes they'll have a question. In a sense, you're presenting yourself there to answer questions that people have, but if they want a long answer, you can politely say, "I'd like to talk with you at some other time about this question, when we have more time." Then make an appointment to talk with them on the phone or get together with them. If they're going to be in the room later on, after you've had a chance to meet everyone, then you can come back and carry on a more lengthy conversation.

When you shake hands or talk with someone, look them in the eye. Don't overdo the eye contact, where a person feels you're intruding into their personal space, but do keep eye contact about fifty or sixty percent of the time you're talking to someone. This lets them know that you're interested, that you're absorbing what they say, and makes a stronger impression than someone who will not look someone else in the eye. As I say, don't be oppressive about it. Don't overdo it or be too intense. Studies show that will not make you popular. Nonetheless, be a good listener and be someone who impresses others as interested in them.

Don't do what some politicians do, who are always looking over the shoulder of the person they're talking to, as if they're looking for someone who's "more important." Each person is important, and concentrate on the one you're talking to at the moment. Let me just add this note to this discussion. It's easy to talk to people you know. It's much harder to talk to people you don't know. It's easier to talk to people you think like you. It's harder to talk to people you think may *not* like you. But in this business of politics, you've got to go against the grain. You've got to go against normal instincts, which tell you to huddle with those you like or know. Instead, reach out. I think you can safely assume that the people who know you best, and are your friends, are on your side and are going to vote for you. Don't overlook them. Don't take them for granted, but once you've talked to them about your candidacy, once you know they're supportive, make sure that both you and they understand it's your job to reach out to others.

Another suggestion is not to assume that people you think are for your opponent are automatically going to be. You may know that someone is of the religion of your opponent, or lives on the same street. I think you can take the attitude very positively that you want to carry your message wherever you can. Many times, even if those I've mentioned do support your opponent, you will make a good impression by treating them as you would anyone else. Maybe they would think that you might be a better candidate. Maybe they do have some reservations about the opponent. Don't assume and write off people who might be potential converts to your cause.

G.   Create A Network

Create a network. There are political party organizations and other groups that can help you. It varies from area to area which groups can help you the most or in what ways they can help you. It depends on what state or community you live in as to how strong these groups are, but almost everywhere it's considered a courtesy to call on your local party committee people or leaders and let them know you are interested in running. Of course if you know them already, from working with party workers and leaders in the past, it certainly will be helpful. Perhaps you are running because a community or party leader asked you to, in which they have "recruited" you as a candidate. The reason for this is that you want to create a network of people who will talk to others about your candidacy favorably. One of the best ways to do this is to <u>tap into existing organized groups</u>, especially those with an inherent interest in public office elections, the primary one of which is usually the political party.

The party leaders and workers are interested in political ideas and candidates year in and year out, and they can really be a big help to a candidate for election, re-election or prospective candidates because they've been through many elections and know the ropes. If you live in an area where the party workers are active, they may be the most important people to help your campaign. Even if you're running in a nonpartisan election, often the party activists are also involved heavily, sometimes behind the scenes, or at least know where to point you for help.

Don't forget what we've discussed already as far as recruiting volunteers. Go over your directories and lists of groups and friends and, whether they are working on your campaign or not, they can certainly become part of your extended network of people who talk about you favorably in the normal course of day-to-day communications with their family, friends, and co-workers. Think of groups like your service clubs, your church, your neighborhood groups, professional or trade associations. You'll want to specifically work on groups which have an active or continuous interest in public issues, such as civic clubs, chambers of commerce or good government associations. If you can meet with the boards or membership meetings of these groups, hopefully you'll gain their endorsement or support. You can gain an extended network of people who already have an existing chain of groups, in addition to those which you are building yourself. Think of it as a grapevine working in your favor, with lots of branches.

Keep in mind that everything you can do to reinforce what you are doing in other areas of the campaign, such as advertising or visiting, will gain maximum impact if it is supported by the personal reference of people known and

respected by those who hear from them about you. There is
something about hearing the same thing from two or three
different channels that strengthens, or as the theorists say,
legitimizes, your message.

H.   Feel At Home Wherever You Are

Feel at home wherever you are. On any given day in a
campaign you may be speaking to several different audiences. Try to approach each group with a fresh attitude. Try
to convey the sense that you feel at home no matter where
you are and that you can establish a relationship with that
person or group that is unique. The most successful political
candidates that I have known, and the public officials who
succeed, have an adaptive sense in which they fit into their
surroundings easily. I remember a candidate who would
always tell those assembled to hear him, in country clubs
or large private residences, how he really felt comfortable
with them, unlike the church basements and union halls he
often visited. The clear implication was that he didn't feel
comfortable anywhere else. Well, that candidate lost. I don't
mean that he wasn't perfectly sincere when he said what he
did, but it betrayed a sense of condescension that probably
came through when he was in other places, even though he
might not have said anything.

So I'm suggesting that you find the things to appreciate in
each place, which will allow you to talk with the people and
let them know that you do feel at home. In my county I have
always run well in the farming areas even though I come
from the more suburban part of the county. I don't wear over-
alls or try to show a lot of in-depth knowledge of agriculture

I don't have, but I try to have a sense of appreciation for what farm families go through, an inquisitive attitude about their work and ask what I could do or should know to help them. A willingness to go out in their areas and be with them on their own home turf means a lot to people.

Of course as a candidate, what you will experience that most people don't, is within a short span of time going into several completely different environments. That's where you have to be relaxed and adaptable so that you can move from a corporate board room, where you may be meeting executives on the one hand, to go out to the shop to meet with the workers or to the union hall to meet with the shop steward. Or to go from the fancy restaurant where the Rotary Club meets to the fire hall dining room, and from there to an ethnic club bar. Of course, in each one of these places you will want to maintain your same message, your same personality, but try to express your message in a way that will get through most clearly to that particular group.

You might want to go on at more length in some places and keep it short in others. You may want to concentrate on the social part of politics, shaking hands, small talk, in some of these settings, whereas in others a prepared talk may be more appropriate. I can't give you the entire answer to this other than to say try to develop a feel for what is appropriate. Some places will welcome you giving out your pamphlets. In other places they will view it as an intrusion. Don't be reticent to ask a member of the group who is your friend, or who has sponsored your visit, about what his suggestions are about the best way to deal with a group. It's better to ask and find out the best approach than to find out later you did the wrong thing. Your aim is to create a common bond, a sense of humanity to reach across any differences you have, whether they be racial or religious, class or politics, your background or the side of town you live on.

If we think about it, it is amusing how we all tend to get in a social groove and to stay there, unless we are in a position like politics in which we can cross these lines. Really it's one of the things I find fun and interesting about politics because it allows you to learn about so many other groups and people with whom you wouldn't otherwise come in contact. One thing I caution against is saying different things to different groups, especially if they are on opposed questions, such as saying one thing to management and another to labor or telling groups in two different sides of town that theirs would be the first neighborhood to get a new park. These things have a way of getting around, whether it is in the press or by word of mouth, and they can come back to haunt you. Even presidential candidates who campaign in different states these days with the electronic media can't do what they used to do and say different things in different states. If they can't do it in the nation, you certainly can't do it in state, county or town.

If you're going into a meeting and you don't know who is in charge or who to talk to, ask somebody to identify the leaders. One way to make the best contact with the group is to know or find out who the leaders are, and talk to them and often they in turn will introduce you to the other members of the group. If you're lucky you may have a friend who is a leader or an officer in such a group, but even if not the leader should be the one to introduce you. Make sure you don't offend the leaders in the group. You and your friend or acquaintance within the group can get a feel for that by talking with the leaders when you enter the room.

I always find that after I go to an event that I have a use for small, handwritten notes. Whenever I go into a campaign I order these note cards to be printed up with my name, address, email address and phone number, a little larger than an index card size and which fits easily into a business sized envelope, that you can send out almost immediately after the event so it's fresh in your mind. The people you would send them to include anybody who had anything to do with an event and making it a success. The people who arranged it, the frontrunners who helped set it up for you in the process, and the leaders of the group, to help you express your appreciation, and really anyone who helped in your visit. I don't keep a record of these memos during a campaign. I just dash them off quickly. What you say is often very predictable but people appreciate the fact that you did them and that you did them yourself. You'd be amazed how many of these notes you can dash off in five minutes or so. Try to keep the things you need to write the notes handy and do it whenever you can, if possible immediately after the event. I've been struck in my recent reading in the history of politics how often handwritten or personal letters have been used by successful candidates.

Although we have new ways of reaching people today I think often a note is more effective even than a phone call. Remember also when you go to events to have a pen and a piece of paper or a notebook or PDA to take notes on things people ask you to do for them, which may be minor things, usually getting pieces of information for them. Or sometimes you can send them an article or a piece of information that you've come across about a pet interest of theirs that has been identified in their conversation. Give out a volunteer card or give someone a candidate business card even if you decided an event is not suitable for a brochure or other piece of literature, this will be helpful. Even a regular business card with information about yourself and your candidacy will leave an impression on people that they can accept just as with any other business or social event.

One of the things that you will discover is that your constituents are an endless variety of interests and viewpoints. The more you can get a sense of your constituency the better off you are. One of the things that you can do as a politician is to pull groups together or to convey from one group to another what their common bonds are. Or put people together who may have similar interests but who may not have known each other. In my opinion, <u>one of the key ingredients of politics is learning to think how other people think</u>. It doesn't mean that you agree with them or that you will always know what is on other people's minds but it means that whether it is your opponent, an interest group or someone who wants to buttonhole you about a topic, or a reporter, try to be able to view things from the other fellow's perspective. Try to think what you would do if you were in their shoes and it will help you understand their actions. This is not a bad idea in life in general, but it certainly has an application in politics where you're dealing with so many people and often people with opposing or competing points of view.

Don't try to be all things to all people. Don't seem to be fawning over every person you meet or every group you speak to or the reaction instead of being positive will be negative. And don't seem to succumb to pressure a group may use in trying to put you on the spot. If you are a business-oriented candidate and you go to speak to a union, or the reverse and appear to be pandering to the group when it can be readily learned that you haven't been that sympathetic to their causes, you would be far better off to go in with a businesslike attitude which says in manner and perhaps in words, "We may not agree on everything but I'm looking for a way to reach out to you as I hope you are to me." What I'm describing may be a little tricky and it is not always easy to try to reach out without appearing to be reaching too far.

I've always found a good rule in politics to be that you <u>assume everything you say, privately, confidentially to your own supporters, or to editors, lobbyists or voters, is going to eventually be known by everybody.</u> It isn't a bad assumption even though it doesn't always come true. It does come true often enough that it's a pretty good premise. Remember, you are in the public eye and what may have seemed to you to be private to you as a private citizen may not necessarily be private to you when you are in the public eye. Anything you say or do is potentially going to be found on the front page of your newspaper.

Chapter Six

Grassroots Campaigning Through Voter Contact

Canvassing + Telephoning + Direct Mail

Our next chapter is grassroots campaigning through voter contact. People to people is still the way that politics is performed even with all our modern technology. In this chapter, we'll cover canvassing, telephoning and direct mail.

We've discussed your strategy but now we need to discuss your **tactics**. Tactics is the way you put your goals and strategies into practical effect, where the rubber meets the road. We'll be talking about the ultimate objective of an election campaign, the voters and how to reach them at the grassroots level through canvassing, telephoning, direct mail.

A. Canvassing

First **canvassing.** Have you ever heard the term "canvassing" used this way before? It's a somewhat old-fashioned term that comes from the use of the term canvas meaning to cover. In other words, to identify your entire area and make a plan for covering it and reaching the people in it. Party workers used to do this regularly, although in my opinion, canvassing is an art that is somewhat going out of style. It will never go out of use to the hardworking candidate. Another term for canvassing might be knocking on doors, going out using your voters list to go to the homes where there are voters (and if it's in a primary, usually those of your political party) to call on them and ask for their vote.

Do you think that is something you would have a hard time doing? Many people are quite shy, especially the first time they go up to a door. Knock. And when the door opens and someone says, "Yes?" You say, "I'm John Smith. I'm running for City Council and I would appreciate your support." I still remember the first time I did this. It wasn't easy. But once I did it and then did it two or three more times, I really came to enjoy it. And you know, I think you'll enjoy it too. It isn't something most of us ever would do except for our desire to run to win.

After all, this is grassroots politics in its raw basic form; one-on-one with somebody who wants to be elected and somebody who can help them get elected if they decide to go their way. If you're not sure if you would enjoy going door to door and asking people for their votes, after you've had a chance to get used to it, I think you'd have to question whether or not politics is something that you will find rewarding. After all, it isn't the "glory" or recognition that may come with being elected to office that determines whether or not you will be successful.

<u>Look at it this way; if you could talk personally to every voter who could vote for you in your jurisdiction, your town, city, county or district and ask them for their vote, don't you think you'd win?</u> I bet you would. Maybe if your opponent did the same thing, then you would be fighting equally and the decision would be made for reasons other than whether or not you had called on someone to ask for their vote, because you would both have called on the same number of people. Chances are though, if you go out and work hard at canvassing, you will have done more than your opponent with the resulting political success. Leave each person you call on with the impression you are running to win. Candidates have to use their time wisely. If you're campaigning in a small community, you may make a main tactic to call on people in their homes. My suggestion would be in today's society, not to try to reach them at home during the day since very few people are home and even those who are homemakers may be out doing errands. I suggest you start around dinnertime; say 5:30 or 6:00 and knock on doors for about two or three hours. Depending on your neighborhood, I'd think 8 p.m. is about as late as you can call comfortably without seeming to intrude on their private or family time.

If you plan your day carefully, you can shake a lot of hands by knocking on doors in the neighborhoods of your district or your city during that period of time. In fact, many candidates I've known who were successful in this type of election, attribute their success to the fact they actually went out and met people in their homes. Don't take a lot of time in any one home. In fact, my suggestion would be not to go inside, even when people invite you in, other than perhaps for a quick minute but to keep moving on. Your goal is meeting people and having them remember your name. Leave them a brochure so that they can read further about you but keep moving. There's always someone who will bog you down with lengthy questions about the details of some policy or some issue in which they are deeply interested. You must learn to be polite on the one hand and yet keep your eye on the goal of meeting as many people as possible on the other.

To maximize your effectiveness when knocking on doors, you may want to have a brochure that you can leave behind. We've already talked about your brochure and what it contains. It will give people the details you may not be able to give them in a lengthy conversation. Some people have suggested that leaving doorknob hangers is a good idea. I tend not to like that because it advertises the fact that someone is not home and many people resent that in today's society. I think it's much better to simply slip your brochure under the door or by the mailbox if no one is home. If you know them or want to personalize the literature that you leave even if you don't know them, then write in advance on a certain number of your brochures, "Sorry I missed you. John." Or words to that effect. It personalizes what otherwise might be just another printed message. Nonetheless, the fact that you were there is the most important thing, even if you didn't get to say hello in person, you made the effort to go to their home. Meeting people and shaking hands is the desired objective and will have the most impact. But if you can't do that, make sure your message lingers through another means.

B.   Telephoning

Telephoning. Let's talk about phone banks. Telephone banks are called that because often during a campaign, especially a large campaign, a number of phones will be installed in a group or bank as they are called and then phone calls can be made by people working with a group approach. In many smaller races, you can have what is in effect a telephone bank by some other techniques.

One of them is called hostess phoning and what that really means is, especially if a family has two or three phones, or with cell phones, someone will have two or three friends in and they can make phone calls from a home on your behalf. You'd be surprised how many phone calls can be made, even from one phone. If someone works at it continuously (as long as you are in the local service area for your telephone and no additional charges are made for calling) even one phone can serve the purpose of a phone bank.

What do you need to make a telephone operation work? The first thing you need to decide is, what are the purposes for your phone bank? In a concentrated telephone operation, there are three different purposes. The first is for **getting people to register to vote.** Usually the deadline for registration is 30 days prior to the election, depending on your state law, so you're phoning for registration must be done before that. It may not be too early to try to influence people as well to vote at that point for your candidacy. In that case, you can combine a registration call with the next type, the **advocacy** call. Advocacy is promoting your candidacy, perhaps as simply as saying to the caller, "We hope you'll be voting for Jane Smith on November 3rd." The third type of call after registration and advocacy is the so-called **"Get out the vote"** message. These calls would be made in the days immediately prior to Election Day or even on Election Day itself, and we'll discuss that more later.

You as a candidate are normally entitled to have a list of all the voters in your area. One of the things that you can do with the list is to get the telephone numbers for them. In some cases, the telephone numbers may be provided with the list, either because the courthouse or your political party collects them, or because you have had volunteers who could take some time at the beginning of the campaign add the telephone numbers to the list. Then you can use that list to do each of the three kinds of phoning. Registration, advocacy and get out the vote. If you ask people who they are for when you do your advocacy calls, then that is called identification and you can use that list later, so marked, for your get out the vote calls to get your supporters to the polls.

A telephone bank takes a lot of commitment from a lot of people. Not everyone likes to call strangers on the phone, but you'll find that there are some people who especially, once they have gotten the hang of it, will actually enjoy it and some will even love it. There are some "naturals" who take to phoning like a duck to water and who can do wonders for you on the telephone. Don't be afraid of offending some people by your telephoning. If you can write a well designed and tested script, you will find that most people, especially if your call is short, to the point, polite and informative, will feel that the phone call has done them a favor. It doesn't have to be the candidate himself who calls, although maybe in a small election, it could be the candidate.

But it can also be someone calling on behalf of the candidate using their best persuasive voice, their best friendly manner. They should discuss how they know the candidate and why he or she is the best possible choice. One of the things about a phone bank that is sometimes not understood, is that people enjoy working together on a phone bank. Suppose you get a rejection when you call someone or they use foul language or hang-up on you and say, "I don't like John Smith and I'm going to vote for his opponent." Or purposely tries to make you feel bad. It doesn't happen a lot but it does happen. Wouldn't you feel a lot better if there was someone there to whom you could talk about it and laugh rather than just sitting there hanging up the phone and feeling negative? Also, you'd be surprised how many times people want to know things and you're far more likely to get the answer if there are two or three people working together.

Phoning for a long time is a little exhausting. It's better to have perhaps two or three people making the calls, while another one may be resting or looking up phone numbers or making sure those making the calls are getting information and refreshments they need. If people whom you call want further information, send them a brochure with envelopes addressed right on the spot. In other words, even a small telephone bank should be a group operation if at all possible.

You may find there are some individuals who want lists that they can call at home by themselves, especially if they are homebound and certainly take advantage of them. However, I think you'll find that once you start sending lists out with people, it's much harder to keep track of them, much harder to get the results and to gain the information from the calling. Sometimes the lists will never come back and the people will just not be able to fulfill what they might have thought they could do.

So my summary is this, especially in a small phone bank, keep close control. Do it on a regular basis so that people can predict their schedules. Keep accurate tabulations of the results, especially if you have decided to call back those who are identified as favorable to turn them out with your get out the vote calls.

To develop and test your script (the text that tells people what to say when they're on the phone) when you first are ready to get your phone operation up and running, have somebody call for one evening using your proposed script with one or two people, especially those who have been involved in planning the phone bank. Then have them criticize, question and analyze the results of the evening's phoning so that you can tighten up the script and smooth out the rough spots in it.

Planning a telephone bank takes a while and it should be assigned to a telephone chairman early if you are going to use it for any of the three purposes, especially if you are using it to call on Election Day.

Today it has become popular to use the technique of "robo-calling," that is using a computer program to make automated calls with a pre-recorded message that the person receiving the call simply listens to. It has some advantages such as obviously reducing the number of people that you need to make calls. It allows you to make a pre-recorded message and to reach a number of homes in a short period of time. You can get a notable person who's well-known and popular, such as an elected official or community leader, to record a message for you and leave that on your behalf. The downside of robo-calling is that people immediately recognize it for what it is, a mechanical substitute for a real person on the phone. In a smaller race, you may not need to or want to use robo-calling. But if your district is larger or you want to get an endorsement that's been made out widely quickly, consider it. Also if some campaign development occurs that needs immediate widespread dissemination, robo-calling allows you to do that. An example would be an opposition mail piece or phone calling operation that is spreading information or making claims that you want to quickly rebut. Even if you have a regular phone operation going, with people, it doesn't hurt to have robo-calling as a supplement. Get out the vote calls also can be done on Election Day if all the workers are out at the polls, and these robo-calls can be done using the marked phone list developed earlier with advocacy and identification calls.

C. Direct Mail

Direct mail. A very important form of voter contact is direct mail. We've talked about canvassing by you and your supporters. We've talked about phone banks by you and your supporters. And now we want to talk about mail. In some ways, mail gives you a way to do in today's world—reaching all potential voters—what at one time was done by canvassing by party workers and by campaign supporters. It has become harder and harder to get messages through to people in today's busy world. People move more often. People work further from their homes. They live in sprawling suburbs. More people are working and they want more time with their families, so that the neighborhood basis of politics has been harder to maintain, especially when it comes to individuals going out in face-to-face contact with their neighborhoods.

One way you have of dealing with this, even if you're attempting to cope with it by canvassing and telephone, is to use the system that has already been set up by the postal service and allows you into all the homes in your district, even if you can't visit them. **There are many experienced campaigners in politics today who feel that direct mail is the most important form of voter contact.** More important than other forms of advertising you might choose. I tend to agree. At a minimum, you will want to consider having a mailing to every household (not every voter since there are often two or more in a household) in the area in which you are running. It may be the most widely communicated aspect of your campaign. It is somewhat expensive but not too much so, in relation to other forms of communicating your message.

What I would suggest is a letter accompanied by your best brochure. Or sometimes the logistics and costs can be reduced by simply having your brochure designed as a "self-mailer," as we discussed in the previous discussion of materials. If you are in a smaller jurisdiction, perhaps you will want to make the letter or mailing piece more personal and local. You can design your mailing or mailings separately from your brochure, although obviously you will want to use your recurring themes. Sometimes a mailing will just be about one aspect of your campaign to draw attention to it. And if you remember our discussion of "negative" or comparison campaigning mailings are sometimes turned into mailings and counter mailings by both sides.

You will want to do a main mailing which would probably be aimed at arriving around ten days to a week prior to the election. You might also want to have specifically targeted mailings to groups with special interests. If you have enough money, you might want to make an upfront mailing to voters or at least to selected groups of voters early in the campaign; perhaps three weeks to a month prior to the election.

In addition to sending a letter from you as the candidate, you might want to have your campaign chairman or some other notable personality, a respected office holder, perhaps a community leader or even a sports figure, send out a letter on your behalf. You might want to send mail to members of the opposition party or others who might be receiving your opponent's message to offset and make positive identification for your own candidacy.

Whenever possible in my campaigns, especially at the local level, I obtained lists of groups such as bankers, dentists, doctors, realtors, farmers and other similar identifiable groups and I asked a leading member of that group who was publicly committed to me, to send a letter identifying me as someone who is knowledgeable and concerned about issues that effect that group to its members. Sometimes that group may not have any particular issue that affects your race, but nonetheless, hearing from someone who is a fellow member of a profession or group will assure them that you are a good candidate to support.

Because you can obtain a list of voters and in many cases a CD or other form of data base from your election office, it will give you the start to your mailing campaign. Remember, often you can order preprinted labels. You can also in many cases, obtain further information about the names that are on the list such as how often voters have voted in the past.

If your resources are limited in terms of how much you can afford to buy in the way of lists to mail, then you may well want to trim the number of names down that you order. First you can do it by households, if people have the same address, eliminating family member duplication. Next you might select those who tend to vote most often and eliminate the ones who vote the least often. Remember, with direct mail, you have to be very careful with your cost projections, the postage costs and of course, observing the deadlines and postal rules for printing your letter and all the associated printing materials.

I am a strong supporter of direct mail. It reaches voters in a personal way and allows you to communicate your message very directly to a voter and those members of the household who will read and see that literature. Remember, the more channels you use, the more effective you will be. If someone gets a letter from you, and a phone call and someone stops at their door, that is a powerful array of voter contact influences. Work hard on designing a good letter. Maybe your printer can help you with format and your workers and advisors can help you design a letter that best reflects your message. <u>Think of that letter as conveying the very essence of your candidacy; the message you would like someone to read if you don't get the chance to talk directly to them.</u>

Chapter Seven

Election Day

**Organizing + Workers + Materials + Working
the Polls + Get Out the Vote + Rovers +
Ads, Absentee Ballots, Transportation**

You've organized your campaign, you've implemented the
ideas, you've recruited your volunteers, you've presented
yourself well, you've done all the campaigning that you can,
so it's all up to the voters, right? Wrong! Election Day is the
day when you make all your sales, and even though in some
states you can now mail in ballots ahead of time, for most
people it's still Election Day when they go to the polls. In this
chapter we're going to look at the organization, the tasks and
training for you and your workers on Election Day.

A.   Organizing for Election Day

One of the first principles we established in this book is
that in politics all the sales are made on one day. I have
tried to emphasize that throughout because it's the constant

goal toward which our efforts are directed. Ironically many candidates forget this as they go along through the hurly burly of a campaign and get quite involved in the day to day challenges of pressures and events.

Election Day requires a very special and sustained effort. Many candidates approach the election day period in a state of exhaustion because they are treating Election Day as a kind of finish line across which they must stagger, rather than as a complete event unto itself, requiring its own energy, its own activity, and for which planning must begin at the very origin of the campaign. I know at this point it may sound redundant, but one of the first things you should do in your campaign is appoint an Election Day coordinator. Although that person may be tempted during the campaign to become involved with many other things, their main objective should be throughout to be lining up people, laying out plans, and thinking about how to treat that Election Day period as the harvesting time for all the hard work that has gone on before.

So the first point is, appoint an Election Day coordinator early and don't let them drop the ball at any point. What is the Election Day coordinator's job? It is to implement the decisions that you make, along with your campaign helpers. First, establish a personnel plan for every voting district or precinct that you have. One of the things that you should obtain very early is a list of all the polling places, their physical locations and a detailed precinct map if it's available in your county, district or your city so that you can begin to get a sense of the territory that you will have to cover. If you are working with an organization of people who know the precincts in your area intimately than you're in luck. If, for example, you are working with party committee people or an established organization with workers throughout the voting districts, then you have the beginning of your organization right there.

If you're starting from scratch, it means that you have to use your volunteer list to find the people who live in the precincts or live close to them which you will have to cover. You will also have to determine, in conjunction with your earlier targeting, which precincts are those that have most priority. To do this you need some knowledge of how you are doing as a candidate in the various areas. The aim, of course, is to reach every voter one more time in addition to all the times you may have reached them already, just before they actually go in to use the polling booth. That means you need the people in every precinct to do it; your Election Day workers. There are many tasks to be done on Election Day, but there is none more important than the people who will actually stand as the voter enters the polling place and who will do the contact work that you need on Election Day.

It is essential to note that many people will be arriving at the polls not knowing how they will vote. That probably seems a little strange to you, since you are interested in politics, and used to looking at candidates prior to elections, talking about them with others, reading about them and trying to determine your best vote. There are many people who do vote but who are not closely attuned to the process. In fact, there are probably more people are like that than there are who closely follow elections! The people who fall in this category probably number 30-40% of the voters. It's a substantial enough proportion of people to tip the balance in an election one way or the other.

B.   Election Day Workers

Another priority of the Election Day coordinator is to train and instruct the workers as to what they will be doing on Election Day. Sometimes workers are recruited and then sent out to do their work without understanding their mission. If that happens their effectiveness will be greatly reduced. That's why if the campaign Election Day coordinator starts early enough, they can really invest the time in training, planning and preparing for the day on which the cash register rings up all your sales. The training should take place on the weekend before the election in the headquarters or other meeting place, perhaps Sunday evening, and materials can be given out and instructions for communicating conveyed. Also for those who may be unfamiliar with the poll worker tasks, there can be a question and answer period, and it is not a bad idea to do some role-playing for how the worker should interact with the potential voter in the friendliest and most positive way.

What do your workers do? In the first place, when they arrive at the polling place in the morning, usually at 7 a.m. but it may vary in your area, they do several things. Hopefully they arrive early so that they can put up posters and check the general layout of the polling place. If they know the area than they will be familiar with what should be in place, if not than they should arrive even earlier, perhaps 20 minutes to a half hour prior to the polls opening. If they are considered "poll watchers," depending on how it works in your state, they are permitted to check out the voting devices, whatever they may be, to verify that they are accessible and that whatever kind of instrument is used for voting that it is in the proper condition. They can also introduce themselves to the election

115

officials and this will give them a chance to make sure that the election officials who are in charge of the polling place know who they are, and that they as workers for you, will be cooperative in their work throughout the day.

One note I should make here is that sometimes election officials are also actively involved in the political process. Sometimes that might be in your favor if they are for you or your candidate, other times it may be that you have to be alert to the sympathy that may lay with another candidate. I have found that most election officials, even though active in politics, are able to separate their own views from their commitment to the fairness of the process, their job. Hopefully they will be committed to a fair count, but is something which you as an advocate for your candidate or your candidacy have to keep in mind. The worker should have a phone so that they can communicate with your headquarters. One of the first things a worker should do after establishing his or her presence at the poll, is to check in with your central phone number, whether it's your home or your headquarters where someone will man the phone, to receive calls from all precincts. Of course a phone at the precinct is essential if something goes awry that you want to be able to communicate very quickly to the central phone number; example, if a poll worker needs more literature then whoever gets that call should be able to dispatch someone with literature or run it over themselves. On the other hand, sometimes it would be a complaint about a supporter being treated unfairly, or someone being deprived of the right to vote. Then the person who gets the call will have to know the procedures to go through to deal with that particular problem.

The main purpose of the campaign poll worker is to establish a presence that makes sure that voters know the message of voting for John Smith.

C.   Message and Materials

Remember when we ordered our literature, one of the things the Election Day coordinator should do is to be involved in those early decisions about how much and what type of literature to order from the printer. One danger in ordering literature early is that sometimes Election Day is forgotten. It isn't all the posters you can put up between the beginning of the campaign and Election Day that count, unless there are also posters up on Election Day itself at the polling place where people vote.

Much of your early activity is designed to reach a smaller group of people who are actively involved at a much earlier point in the process. Strangely enough the cumulative effect of all the pre-election day work may still not be enough, and requires an intense activity at the tail end to catch all those people who need to be reached to guarantee a majority. What is the best way to do this? Make sure your posters are up. Make sure they are up in visible places as you approach the poll. Probably you should allow three to four posters for each polling place and have a distribution system for getting them out to the poll workers prior to Election Day. The same thing applies to handout literature, make sure you have enough. Mainly what you should have would be the handout cards we described previously. One of the things we mentioned was to have a handout card with your picture, primarily with your name and the office you are running for. You should also have available pamphlets or brochures with more extensive information for those who have the time to read them or who ask for them specifically.

If voters have to stand in line, which sometimes happens, they may be bored and often that will be a time when they will read more extensive literature, but if, as usually happens, they are walking directly into the polling place, chances are it is the name that will mean the most. What you want your workers to do is position themselves in a place where they will see or be able to talk to or shake hands with every voter who comes into the polling place. That's not always easy, especially if experienced people and those who know the precinct well decide to try to set themselves up in the same spot. If there are many candidates who have workers at a particular polling place, what seems like a small crowd may develop around the entrance to the polling place. But you can't let that deter you or your workers. There's a job to be done, if you are doing it against competition, well that's what politics is all about. Hopefully you can establish a friendly relationship with the other people who are at the polling place. Do not have hard feelings even with those who are working for your opponents. Oftentimes this may seem hard with the tension of the campaign and the finality of the decision approaching and emotions may run high.

Certainly for you the candidate, this is a day where you can be forgiven if you are nervous or intensely concerned, but don't overdo it. Try to be relaxed and confident. Use your efforts right up until the close of the election. When you or your worker have established your spot and you have your literature, you should have a pin on or a large button that allows people to see visually who you are for and you can reinforce it verbally by saying to each voter something along the line of, "We are supporting Jane Smith for County Commissioner." Hand the card to them, smile and get ready for the next person. Generally don't get involved in conversations with people other than the exchange of a few sentences. Most people will not try to engage you in such a conversation because they will be intent on getting in to vote.

D.   Working The Polls

Some people even resent the fact that there are campaign workers or candidates outside a polling place, but there's nothing you can do about this. If they say grumpily, "I know who I'm for," have a friendly response that doesn't seem argumentative but that gets across the point of your candidate such as, "Well in that case I hope it's Jane Smith."

Obviously you the candidate cannot be at every polling place. My suggestion for the candidate is to go to a polling place in which there are many voters, and in particular perhaps a large polling place where your support is not well established. The reason I say this is because your home precinct should be going for you. It is your neighborhood and the people there know you. You might want to have a family member there, or loyal workers whom you have known over the years. They should be able to bring in your precinct, but your presence may make a difference at another precinct and that's where we want to find you.

You may want to circulate between polling places but that might dissipate your efforts. You should probably go to an area that's up for grabs, or where people might be sympathetic to you but haven't had a chance to meet you. Having the candidate at a polling place really changes the equation. It makes people pleased to be able to meet the actual candidate since most times voters don't ever meet the candidates they are voting for. It establishes a strong presence in which you can supersede as a candidate the workers for all your opponents, who are merely after all surrogates for their candidates. Therefore make sure people know you are the candidate and establish your identity that you are the person that the posters and the literature and the buttons describe.

You should extend your hand, smile, identify yourself and say to the voter, "I'm John Smith, I'm running for Town Council, or Mayor, or whatever, and I would like your help and I would like your support. Will you vote for me?" or whatever you're comfortable saying. You should be ready to say it many times over without a sense of boredom or repeating a rote statement. Try to give each new voter your full energy and make sure they get the message. There will people who say, "I don't like you," or, "I'm not for you." Don't let it bother you, shrug it off. Be ready for those and remember it isn't each exchange that wins the election, it's the accumulation of them and that there are always a few people who try to slow you down or discourage you; don't let them do it.

Also don't be intimidated if there are other people at the poll who try to move you or your workers around or tell you that you can't stand in a certain place or can't do certain activities. Don't take orders from an opponent; make sure the authoritative election official runs the poll. Remember there is a law in each state that covers in detail activities at a polling place, and make sure you check that law carefully. If you are doing the job of preparing adequately, you as a candidate and also your campaign workers will spend some time studying these laws and knowing what you can and cannot do at the polling place.

Remember this, having workers at a polling place does not guarantee that you will win that polling place, it just means that your chances will be greatly increased for those who arrive at the polling place and who haven't made up their minds.

There are some polling places where overt activity and aggressive representation of your candidacy are frowned on. I would say that you don't want to be offensive to people whose practices are different from what I have described here, but I also would caution you that what might seem to be resentment on the part of a few people about the way things are done in this precinct, may not really reflect what all voters feel. I found that especially newer or younger voters are very appreciative of the effort you make to help inform them, and involve them by your presence if your manner is polite, non-threatening and not pushy. If you are presenting the message and the candidate that you believe in people really shouldn't resent it. In my opinion it's an important part of the process and the gains you make from good representation at the polls far outweigh any distaste that voters might have.

If someone wants to have a long discussion with you or your worker, you should be very careful not to be distracted. During the light periods of voting perhaps longer conversations are in order. Sometimes when it's slow it's the only way to kill time, but on the other hand for you as the candidate or your workers, it's your job to be greeting everyone and you shouldn't let anyone distract you from that.

E. Get Out The Vote

For the effort which campaigners often refer to as "GOTV," you will need to organize each voting precinct with three or four people and hopefully more than that. In the first place you need your workers as we've already described. It would also be advisable for you to have someone who is checking off the names for you of those who have voted in each precinct. Now if this is done by another polling official or a party worker, you don't have to duplicate it, but if no one does it in your precinct, you normally have the right to have someone sitting at a table where they can either hear people identify themselves or ask them directly. In that way if you have an inside worker with the registration list for your area you can check off those who have voted. Why would you want to do this? Not just for the busy work, but so you can identify those at certain points later in the day who may be your voters and who have not turned out to vote by that time. Again this means that you have to plan ahead and have the list of voters who are for you or who are in your party and their phone numbers to make maximum use of this particular activity. Let me remind you to think back to the section where we talked about phone banks. If you have had an advocacy and identification phone bank in your campaign having that list is only beneficial if it is then used on Election Day to make sure that those who indicated support for you are then urged to vote by telephone. I would suggest that if you are going to make such calls you make them at approximately 4:00 to 6:00 p.m., although of course you can keep it up right until the end.

If you can have workers on your phone bank on Election Day you will greatly magnify the work you have done previously in telephoning. It does mean that not everybody can be manning the polls and that's why when it comes to distributing manpower on Election Day there may be an argument between those who are responsible for the phone bank and those who are responsible for manning the polls, they might be competing for the same workers. Hopefully you have enough volunteers that you will be able to do both jobs adequately.

F.   Rovers

There are other jobs in addition to Election Day poll workers and telephoners, one of them is to be a "rover." A rover is someone who goes between several polls located near each other and who makes sure the workers are there, the signs are up and that all is in order. If you have a small town election it may be that you have only one or a few polling places, in that case the roving may be done by you or your workers between a small number of precincts. If your area of your town, your city or your district covers a large area and has many polling places, than you will want to have someone in overall charge, the Election Eay Coordinator, as we described already, who can then delegate specific responsibility for roving. I would say perhaps 10-15 polling places can be covered by one rover during an Election Day period.

Remember Election Day stretches normally from 7 a.m. until 8 p.m. (in some areas or states it's different hours but you can find that out) and that's a long period of time. If you do not have enough workers to be at each poll during that whole period, then aim to have them there at the busiest periods of voting. In many areas it has gotten to be quite common that the largest voting periods are one push early in the morning, say from 7 a.m. to 8:30 or 9:00 a.m., and then a final push that starts at about 4:00 or 5:00 p.m. and builds up until approximately 7 p.m. and then slacks off a bit until the close of the polls. But there are also areas where steady voting throughout the day is common. If you are standing at the polling place and the people who normally work that polling place are remarking about the heavy number of people in the morning, it is highly likely that throughout the entire day there may be a strong push. In other words there may be a strong interest in that election in the electorate. On a slow election day such as might occur in your race, especially if you are running for a local office, don't be discouraged, you have to reach the people who do appear no matter whether there is a heavy turnout or a light turnout.

The rover's job is to drive from polling place to polling place enthusing, informing, and supporting your workers who are there for your candidacy and making sure that they have coffee, or lunch, or literature, or signs if they need them. Sometimes if you can get one or two loyal workers in a precinct they can do a whole day working for you, but the point should be made it is tough work. It is not easy and not all people are inclined to stand around, sometimes with nothing to do when there aren't many people, and other times being overwhelmed by people all arriving at once. That's why when you recruit your workers please try to let them know that this is an important job, how much you appreciate it and how vital it can be.

As the rover gets to each polling place on their tours they should be looking for trends or listening for information that they may pick up and relay back to your central telephone number. Probably the Election Day Coordinator should remain at the central phone. They are the person who knows where everybody is supposed to be, who should have all the list of polling places and their locations and who would know how to contact the rovers if they have to. By the way, if your central phone number is likely to be busy, there should be two or three alternative phone numbers and people should not be stuck calling a number that is going to be busy all day. You need to get the information out early for your poll workers to give them their instructions and that is part of the coordinator's responsibility. Those instructions should repeat much of the advice that I have given you (perhaps in succinct form) and have the telephone number or numbers where they can call for help. For example, how to call the court house if there is a problem with voting information or individual prospective voters have a problem. These instructions should be gotten to each Election Day worker with their quota of posters and literature, usually three days or more before the election so that it will not be a last minute thing.

That way they will have a chance to count the literature, look it over, and make sure they are ready to get it into their car and to the polling place. A few words about security; remember those who are for your opponent are not anxious for you to get your literature out, so at all times make sure any large quantities of your literature are not left exposed, whether they are being sent out to poll workers before the election, or whether they are being transported or stored on election day itself. When you do not need all the literature that you are going to give out and you are going to stash it somewhere, put it where it is undercover or safe.

When the distribution is given to workers ahead of time it also gives you a way of knowing whether or not all the workers that you hope are going to be working for you. One way you can tell is if you distribute literature to people and it does not appear at the polling place. It may be an immediate tip off that you need to get your own worker at that polling place. You should hold back a certain amount of literature that you will need to plug holes on Election Day. The rovers, for example, should have back up literature, but they should get rid of it all by the end of the day. You don't want any ammunition in your gun after the battle is over. A rover ought to also be able to call your central number, and perhaps if you have to do this, switch people from a poll that may be small to a large precinct, or from a more friendly precinct which you hope will be going for you to a more hostile precinct where you need representation.

G. Ads, Absentee Ballots and Transportation

Should you have ads in the newspapers, on the radio or on television on Election Day? The answer to that is whatever your media plan may be, try to incorporate some last minute advertising on Election Day. If you've been strapped and don't have the money to put into it or it's a choice between doing it before the election or on Election Day, then stress the days before the election. But if you have some media effort that can be made on Election Day itself, it may catch those last minute deciders and it may remind your supporters to go to the polls.

There are things you can do to help boost your vote. One is to make sure that you have taken full advantage of **absentee**

ballot provisions that allow you, prior to the vote, to make sure that your supporters can obtain absentee ballots and get them in by the required time. I am a strong supporter of using absentee ballots. This requires a lot of advance planning. I'd suggest that if possible, when you do a mailing earlier in the campaign, if it's about three weeks before election day, if it is legal in your state (you can find this out from your election official) either send an absentee ballot, or possibly an application for an absentee ballot to all those who might under any circumstances be away. I always try to contact every household since someone might be planning to be away. Remember you would never think of being absent on an election day under normal circumstances, but for many people plans of a business nature or a personal nature take precedence in many cases so that they might not plan their schedule or activities around Election Day even though obviously it's pretty important to you.

Procedures for absentee ballots and other forms of early voting vary from state to state. I can't give you detailed advice here. Suffice it to say you should make it a point in dealing with your election officials to find out well in advance how absentee ballots are obtained, how much you can do as a candidate to promote them and then make sure that you are using this for a valuable way of gaining votes. Many candidates forget about it sometimes to their peril. For example, a recent governor of California was elected because of absentee ballots. The votes for those who voted at polling places would not have supported his victory, but when the absentee ballots were counted, he won. It's a pretty good reminder that absentee ballots can be critical.

Another way you can help yourself at the polls is through **transportation.** If there are people in your area who are for you, but who can't get to the polls, obviously anything you can do by providing drivers for them will be appreciated by them and also will make sure you get your maximum number of votes to the polls. Most party workers in areas where there is a strong party organization will have identified the voters who are known to need transportation help, but it won't hurt if you are making phone calls in your advocacy or identification calls, or your get out the vote calls. If people say they are not able to get to the polls, that's a golden opportunity to step in and provide it. The Election Day coordinator, if possible in this kind of a larger scale campaign, ought to have some cars that he can dispatch if needed to transport people.

Let's recap Election Day. Election Day is the day when you bear fruit from all the work of the election period, and it's critically important. Planning must be done for Election Day well in advance and all the recruiting of people can take a long period of time, but must be done in a deliberate and thorough manner. Those recruited for different jobs such as poll worker, inside worker, or rover must be trained and prepared to do their jobs well. Literature must be ordered in advance so that it is available freely. For posters, brochures, handouts and yard signs, a distribution system must be put in place so that all of these items maybe gotten to those who need them for each poll prior to Election Day. Assignments must be clear to all workers. Alertness to the fairness of the voting operation in each polling place must be stressed. Flexibility in reassigning people, or redistributing literature and posters is a big help. Advertising should be orchestrated to help provide that last kick for your supporters. Coverage of your poll workers must be thorough. Each one of them should be well equipped and motivated to do the things they have to do for you and remember it's that reinforcement with the voters that you are looking for. When you and your workers look the voter in the eye and present the image and the appearance that we have discussed before it's going to win you votes. It's part of the representative process for you to be there meeting the people, asking for their votes on a personal basis, and each worker who does this for you as a surrogate is really saying the same thing, "I'd like your help. I'd like to have the opportunity to serve you."

Chapter Eight

After the Election: Run to Win and Win to Run

Momentum + Analysis, Transition, Reports + Winning to Run

Our last chapter is **running to win and winning to run,** what to do after the election. Remember that you already are a candidate for the next election. And with all the emphasis I have placed on Election Day it would seem like once the election is over,you deserve to rest. Well, that may be true but you are not going to have that chance just yet.

A.   Keep Your Momentum Going

In the first place, don't make plans to go away right after an election. Some people in politics do this, and I have always wondered why. The period right after an election victory is very important in terms of solidifying the gains that you have made. It is the time to thank people, every last one of them, who helped you campaign and win. Take the press calls and have a considered explanation for your victory that lays the groundwork in the minds of those who read or hear it for your assumption of office and your themes being converted into actions and policies.

This is the time to plan a party for those who worked on the campaign, within a short period of time after the election. Win (or lose) people have stories to share and many positive feelings about a campaign, and you of course want to say thank you to all those who have volunteered and spent their time on your campaign and worked so hard for you.

B. Analysis, Transition Into Office, Reports

I don't think it jinxes a campaign to think of what will happen after the election is over. Often analysis of the results is done best when the events are still fresh and this is when you want to look at the areas that supported you strongly and the particular people who did excellent jobs for your in your victory.

It may also be a period when you need to begin planning to assume the job itself. This is often called the "transition" period and it can be pretty important in terms of mastering what is expected of you. There may be decisions you make, if, for example you have to choose staff members, or decide on alignments with other officials elected when you are or who are already in office. There may be people who can advise you about the job but who have been waiting for the uncertainty of the election to get behind you. Now that the "superficial" aspects of a campaign period are over, some of the issues may appear on close inspection to be a bit more difficult to deal with than you had previously thought.

Under normal circumstances being "sworn in" will be a couple of months away. But often there is a lot to be done. Sometimes events may transpire in that period when you are an official "elect" that are going to color your ability to do the job when you get in there. So it may be a time when, if you are going newly into an office, to contact the incumbent or others who are involved in governing the jurisdiction to begin gaining information and getting viewpoints. And make sure your installation in office, whatever the ceremony involved, is sufficiently marked by attendance and celebration with your supporters as your final thanks for their help.

This is also a time when you may have to begin filing reports of a financial nature within a 15 or 30 day period depending on what the law in your jurisdiction says. You may want to review with your treasurer what the bank account looks like, whether all the bills have been paid and whether there is an account balance that you may need for your political activities that continue separately from your official position. So don't slack off, don't let down your guard, don't relax too much.

C. "Winning to Run"

Also just as I encouraged you to run to win, now I am going to turn the tables a little bit and say "win to run." It probably seems pretty premature to you, but at the very moment of victory you should be thinking of whether you want to run again, how to be reelected and what actions you will have to take to provide for your political support while you are in office.

Sometimes candidates feel that once they win an office, it will be easy to stay in office. Well perhaps that is sometimes the case, but I'd say far more people have been surprised that it wasn't the case, than have found that it was so.

Most people who win in office expect to run again and would like to run again and, if they feel they have done a good job, they expect people to support them. But remember when you go into an office you are going to be doing things and taking actions that will create a new political equation. Running from scratch in some ways is easy compared to running when you are an incumbent.

So I guess my point is, even as you assume office, begin to plan the things that will help you remain politically viable and will create a good basis for a future reelection campaign. Politics is a never ending cycle and those who forget that time is always moving by can suddenly be surprised when they reach a reelection time and realize that there are things they should have been doing from the very beginning that they didn't. So when I say win to run that's what I mean.

Conclusion

"Running for a Reason"

As we approach the end of this book, Run to Win!, let me share some thoughts with you from my experiences. Remember, the reason for going into politics is not only to win in office, it is to work for the principles and beliefs you have, and you feel are important for your community. You run for a reason.

Keep that reason in mind as you go throughout the long hard days of the campaign. Let it keep you going, even though you may be engaged in drudgery and the tasks necessary to win, but which sometimes may seem far removed from your goals. Goals are only important if they can be implemented, if they can be put into practice. In our system, you can only put them into practice if you are in a position of responsibility.

I've often found in the positions that I have held that when you are being pressured by the tasks at hand, and by people who want things only their way, the motivation of your beliefs and your philosophy is what can keep you going. It's certainly true of the campaign as well. Remember also, when you do get in office, that all the things that you said in the campaign were not just window dressing, but were your message that people have a right to expect you to try to implement, knowing you may not accomplish every goal or every policy change you want.

In the campaign, don't make promises you can't fulfill, but commit yourself to work toward things that people would like to achieve and that you can articulate for them. I have always been pretty cautious about making promises to do specific things, but I often talk about what I would hope to achieve and the philosophies that I would work for. I think that is what most people expect, unless there's a specific issue that is related to the campaign, and on which you have a clearly understood commitment.

Be action oriented, whether it's in the campaign or in an office that you seek to fulfill. The ability to bring a philosophy to life in practice is so important and very fulfilling. Let's review as a way of wrapping up. You've thought through the process of becoming a candidate and you've committed yourself to run and win. You've established your plan, you've created your organization, you've developed your message and decided how to communicate that message to others. You've done the voter contact programs of a grassroots nature and all the work that goes into telephoning and canvassing and mail. You've worked hard on Election Day to pull it all together. You've done the follow up work and are ready to assume office. When that point comes, I hope you can look back on this book as playing an important role in helping you formulate your strategy and your attack, and that you've been pleased with the decisions you've made.

In the final analysis, people may thank you for being a good candidate. They might thank you for running to represent their views and in office, they may thank you for what you're doing…but don't count on too many thanks. Don't count on a lot of people taking time out of their lives and their own personal agendas to recognize what you've done. Even if you've done a good job, my advice would be that it's far more likely to give you a sense of personal satisfaction, because you know that you've tackled some tough problems and worked hard, than because many people will ever appreciate it. In our system of democracy, with all its advantages, one of the results is, people tend to take for granted what their public officials do and often to criticize them for making decisions that are tough and unpopular.

The fact that you haven't let that stop you makes you part of a select fraternity of public spirited citizens who, when all is said and done, make sure that our system of democracy works. My hat is off to you. I know what you're going through, but for those of us in politics, it isn't just the hard work. It's also the fun and the challenge of running to win!